FURNITURE IN 24 HOURS

FURNITURE IN 24 HOURS

SPIROS ZAKAS

AND HIS STUDENTS AT PARSONS SCHOOL OF DESIGN

PHOTOGRAPHS BY DAVID COX
AND BOGUSLAW KAPUSTO

COLLIER BOOKS

A DIVISION OF MACMILLAN PUBLISHING CO., INC.
NEW YORK

COLLIER MACMILLAN PUBLISHERS

LONDON

Macmillan Publishing Co., Inc.
866 Third Avenue, New York, N.Y. 10022
Collier Macmillan Canada, Ltd.

Library of Congress Cataloging in
Publication Data
Zakas, Spiros.
    Furniture in 24 hours.
    1. Furniture making—Amateurs'
Manuals.   I. Parsons School of Design,
New York.   II. Title.
TT195.Z34   1976   684.1   76-21870
ISBN 0-02-633390-2
ISBN 0-02-082900-0 pbk.

First Collier Books Edition 1976
Third Printing 1977
Furniture in 24 Hours is also published in
a hardcover edition by Macmillan
Publishing Co., Inc.

Printed in the United States of America

THIS BOOK IS DEDICATED TO
ALLEN TATE
WHO STIRRED MY CURIOSITY,
AS A STUDENT,
LIKE A PROPELLER THAT BEGAN
TAKING ME TO OTHER PLACES

CONTENTS

MY SINCERE THANKS TO OLGA CRAIGEN FOR HER DEDICATED WORK
IN MAKING THIS BOOK A REALITY

INTRODUCTION

SPIROS ZAKAS

"Home, Sweet Home" is still a good saying, and everyone's home should be just that way. However, a home can be sweet only if **you** live in it, put **yourself** in it, and enjoy it. The more **you** put into it, the more **you** it will be, so only **you** can create it.

Filling your home with livable furniture is one way of creating your own special environment. A trip to a furniture store would of course accomplish this, but making your own is certainly more economical and infinitely more satisfying. Why buy all ready-made when you can make some of it?

The hardest part is buying the material; making the furniture is fun and easy. Everyone seeks to have unusual and interesting things to share with his or her family and friends, but it's almost impossible to buy custom-made or unique furniture at reasonable prices. When you make your own, you combine technical skills with your own creative talents and it becomes more meaningful.

Most people can't imagine making furniture, but you'll find it is surprisingly easy. Think of it: a chair has a seat and a back; a table has a top and a base. We have detailed the materials and methods so carefully it's as simple as following a recipe.

Once making furniture was a very complicated affair, mainly because the materials and methods that machines have given us were not then available. It was necessary to make intricate dowels and joints, a complex and tedious task. Today there is no need for making strong joints and corners because excellent adhesives can be used. We have at our disposal epoxy, contact cement, resin glues, etc., for strengthening joints and corners. In fact, there are now glues that dry stronger than the material they have joined.

Another complication we don't have to contend with is the old method of upholstering with strappings, springs, and stuffing down. Today soft furniture can be made with polyurethane, polyester, foam rubber, and polystyrene pellets (for beanbag furniture).

Wood is still very much available, and the cost isn't high. In this book we work quite a bit with plywood, which is three or more layers of veneer glued together with the grain flowing in the opposite directions. This makes it almost impossible for the plywood to warp. The result is much stronger and less expensive than solid-core wood panels. Other by-products of wood we use are chip board and Masonite. Chip board is thick, rough, and porous, but sometimes warps. In contrast Masonite is thin, smooth, and nonporous, and tempered Masonite won't warp. Then there is gypsum board, which is a by-product of recycled paper (like thick layers of cardboard glued together). It's not structurally as strong as a flat panel, but when you begin bending it into soft shapes it becomes stronger. You'll be surprised at what you can produce with these materials and 2 x 4s.

We are also fortunate today to have portable tools such as jigsaws, drills, circular saws, sanders, etc. For me, the greatest tool ever made has to be the staple gun. I sometimes think I could build a house with one (I'd like to try!). I always feel tools are a good investment, because there's nothing like having one when you really need it. And they can become incentives to taking care of household repairs—which could even lead to adding on another room. I've seen it happen. Tools can really make a job surprisingly easy.

The purpose of this book was to create an incentive for my students, and to provide them with an opportunity to share with you some of their ideas and ideals. Who knows? one of them could become another Thomas Chippendale, Louis Tiffany, or Frank Lloyd Wright. Every year I have students from all over the world—France, Israel, Japan, Scandinavia, Italy, Hong Kong, etc. We have a meeting of the minds and study design in relation to the past, the future, and to the varied needs of people today.

We all attend Parsons School of Design, which is over seventy-five years old. The school is known internationally for its quality and progressiveness in design. Parsons created (over fifty years ago) the original "Parsons Table," which today is a household word. Many of the world's finest designers have been trained at Parsons, and the school continues to evaluate and reevaluate man's needs, desires, and influences, because man's needs **do** change.

Consider your own "home, sweet home." It is the only place where you can live as you want, with no time clocks, traffic jams, or crowded elevators—and you can **live** as you want, in the **style** you want. It's a place to be **alone** or a place to **share** with your family and friends. There's no need to wait until you can afford to furnish it to suit your life-style. Create your own furnishings by following the directions in this book. You can do it—because we already have.

SEATING

There are many ways to sit—on stools, benches, lounge chairs, love seats, dining chairs, and more. Of course, everyone knows about seating, but not everyone has quite imagined it the way we have. We feel that if you are going to make something, it should be "special" in more ways than one. A chair doesn't really have to be just a chair.

All the materials and methods necessary for construction have been itemized. You may, of course, want your chair bigger or softer or more colorful. Using the basic instructions, you can personalize your furniture project in any way that appeals to you.

Use your imagination in choosing your materials. The best method is to feel the fabrics that you like and pick out your designs and color. You can always repaint a wrong choice.

All options are open to you. Feel free to change our designs to suit your own needs. Once you have the materials together you will be surprised at how easy it is to make these chairs. Enjoy your new furniture—there is nothing that is more fun than creating your own comfort.

TRIANGLE LOUNGE PLATFORMS

MARY HOWARD

Materials

— **five** pieces 5½″-thick foam rubber, each
  3′ x 3′ x 4′ 3″ diagonal triangle
— **five** pieces ¼″-thick plywood, each
  3′ x 3′ x 4′ 3″ diagonal triangle
— **five** pieces fabric, each 48″ x 56″, can
  be different colors
— staples
— glue

Tools

— staple gun
— saw, yardstick, pencil, scissors, unless
  you have foam rubber, plywood, and
  fabric cut out by the suppliers

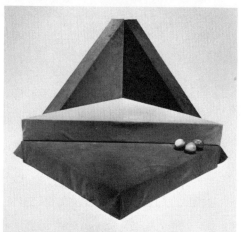

Method

Examine illustrations
— glue each foam-rubber triangle to each
  plywood triangle; let dry
— wrap fabric around each triangle, and
  staple to plywood base
— play with combinations

FABRIC   56″wide × 48″ long

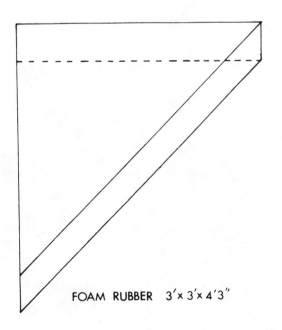

FOAM RUBBER   3′x 3′x 4′3″

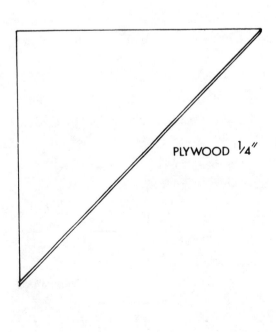

PLYWOOD ¼″

2 E-Z CHAIR

YUTAKA MATSUMOTO

Materials
— **one** piece plywood, ¾'' x 36'' 73''

Tools
— electric drill
— electric saw
— coping saw
— sandpaper

Method
Examine illustrations
— cut plywood with electric saw into **three**
  pieces (sizes shown in drawing) (**one**
  narrow piece is for the seat and the
  other **two** pieces are for the supports)
— using electric drill and electric saw, cut
  15''-diameter circle out of the supporting
  parts
— using electric saw and coping saw,
  make a 15'' slit in each supporting part;
  width of each slit is ¾'' and each slit
  is at 60° angle from surface (top view is
  shown in detail in drawing)
— using sandpaper, make surfaces smooth
— fit the supporting parts together, then
  put the seat in position

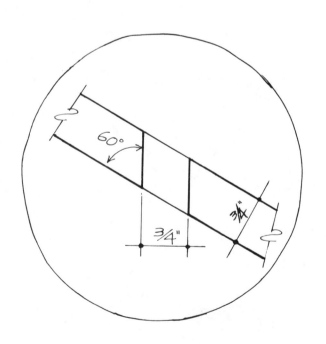

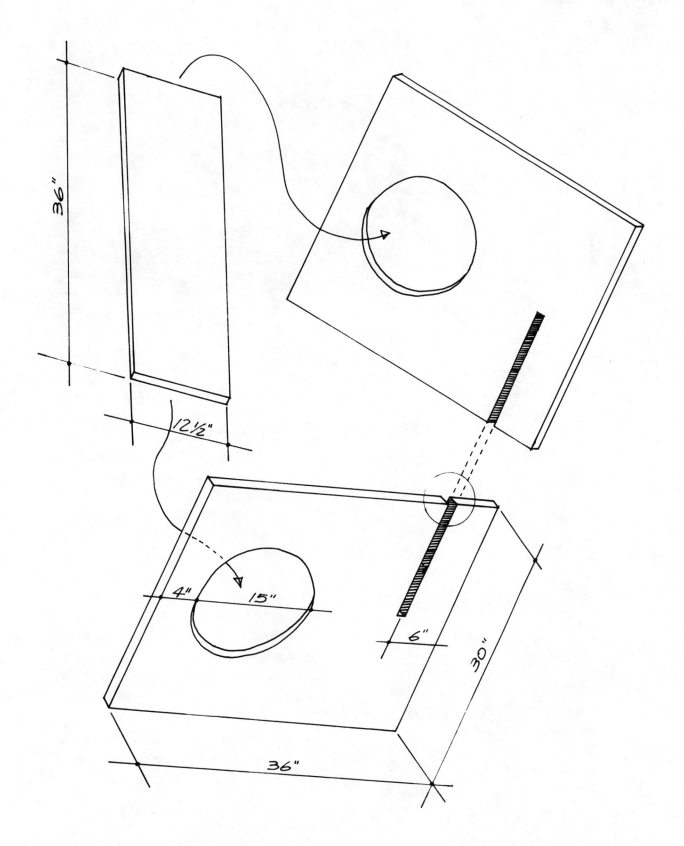

3 BENCH

DEBBIE GOLD

Materials

— **four** pieces white pine, 16" x 3"
— **four** pieces white pine, 32" x 3"
— **four** pieces white pine, 18" x 3"
— 3½ yds. Ultra-suede (45" wide)
— **one** plywood plank, 27¾" x 23¾" x ½"
   foam, 37¾" x 23¾" x 3" thick fabric,
   1 yd. x 45" wide
— **two** 1" eyehooks

Tools

— staple gun
— 3 M Spray Mount
— **two** 38" wood vises
— epoxy glue

Method

See illustrations

— place **two** 32" x 3" pieces of wood along
   with **two** 18" x 3" pieces of wood
   corner to corner to form a rectangle
— insert the **four** 16" x 3" pieces of wood,
   with epoxy on the ends at corners, to
   form legs

— place vises on opposite corners and
   hold in place for 12 hours
— turn bench upside down and place
   remaining pieces of wood (**two** 18" x 3"
   and **two** 32" x 3") in between the
   vertical 16" x 3" pieces of wood
— apply glue to ends of longer wood
— repeat with vises, holding for 12 hours
— cut Ultra-suede (see diagram)
— once pieces are cut, wrap each piece
   around each piece of wood
— once bench is assembled, place the
   foam on plywood plank, using glue to
   secure
— cover with fabric, using staple gun to
   secure to plywood plank (underside of
   plank)
— attach the **two** eyehooks to underside of
   plywood (opposite each other) and
   inside top of bench in order to secure
   bench top to base

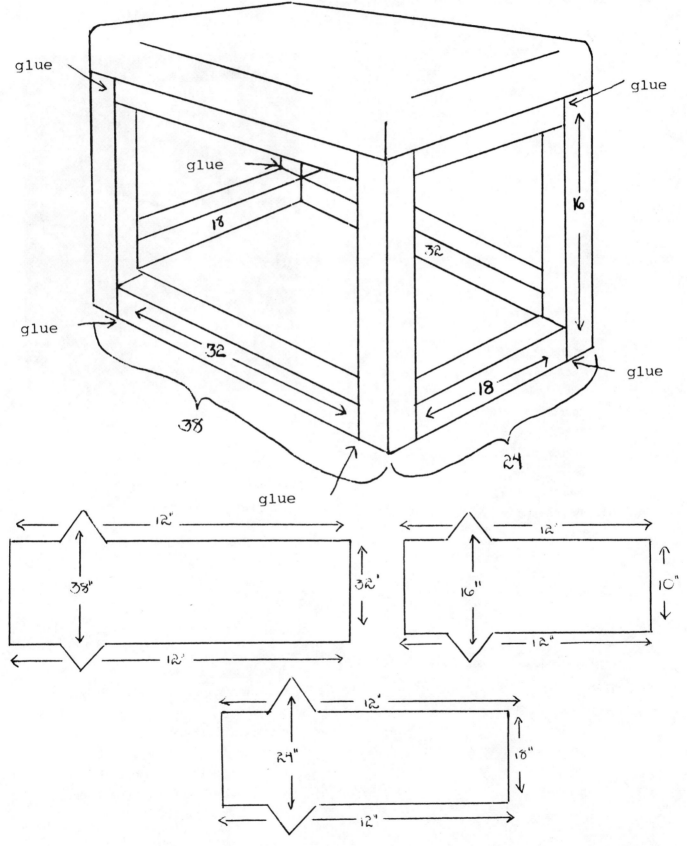

4 SLAB CHAIR

DEE MacDONALD

Materials
— **one** sheet plywood, finished on one side, ½″ x 4′ x 8′
— **eight** oak cleats:
    four cleats 1″ x 2″ x 6″
    two cleats 1″ x 2″ x 6¾″
    two cleats 1″ x 2″ x 7″
— **four** oak cleats:
    two cleats 1″ x 2″ x 6¾″
    two cleats 1″ x 2″ x 7″
— white glue
— **24** finishing nails, 1″ length
— plastic wood
— **one** qt. primer
— **one** qt. acrylic yellow bright paint

Optional
— **four** cushions, make or buy

Tools
— paper, 36″ x 36″
— pencil
— tape
— ruler
— jigsaw
— hammer
— clamps
— sandpaper
— white glue
— ¼″ drill for hole, 1″ hole saw
— brush, 1½″ width
— nail punch
— circle template

Method
Examine illustrations
— draw 2″ grid on paper
— draw design on grid for two side panels of chair
— cut plywood to obtain two 3′ x 3′ pieces
— tape paper to unfinished side of plywood; line up bottom of paper design with edge of wood transfer pattern onto piece of 3′ x 3′ plywood

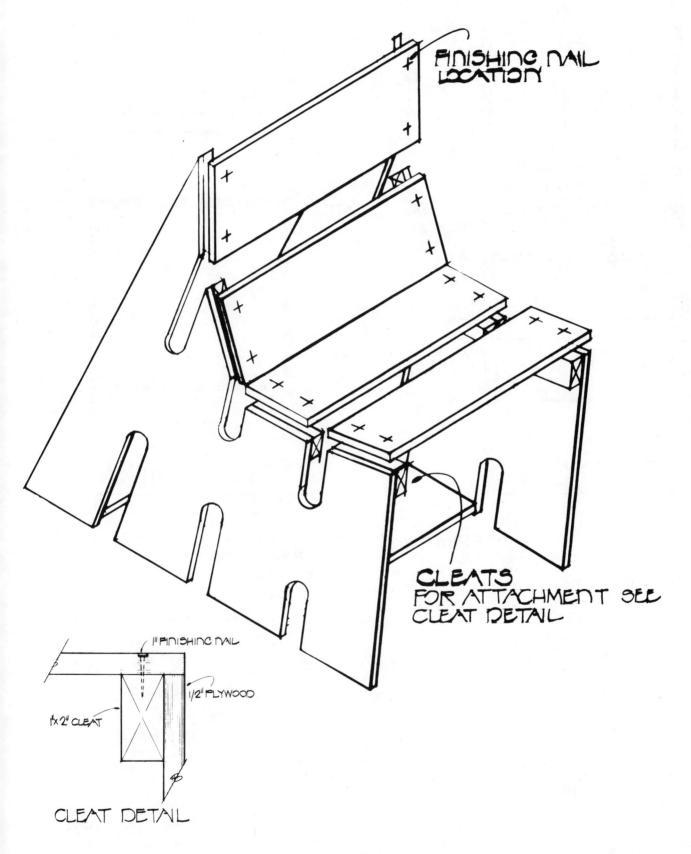

FINISHING NAIL LOCATION

CLEATS FOR ATTACHMENT SEE CLEAT DETAIL

1" FINISHING NAIL

1/2" PLYWOOD

1x2" CLEAT

CLEAT DETAIL

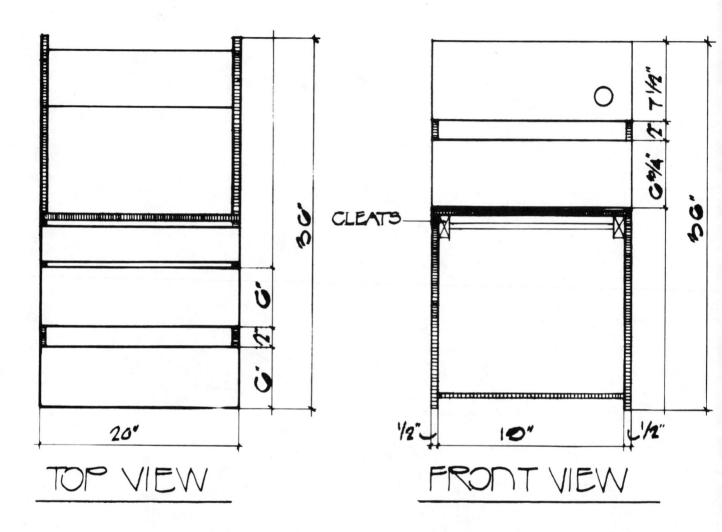

TOP VIEW

FRONT VIEW

— using jigsaw, cut out pattern from wood
— lay patterned wood on second piece of 3' x 3' plywood
— trace pattern onto unfinished side of second piece
— using jigsaw, cut out pattern from plywood
— sand all edges
— from remaining plywood, cut out **six** pieces:

7½'' x 20''	6¾ '' x 19''
6¾'' x 20''	7'' x 19''
6'' x 20''	6'' x 20''

— sand edges

— glue **eight** oak cleats to matching edges of both top side panels
— glue **four** oak cleats to matching bottom panels
— clamp, let dry
— use hole saw with circle template to make 1'' hole in bottom right-hand corner of top slate
— one by one, fit slates into matching position and nail into cleats
— with nail punch, countersink nails
— fill holes with plastic wood
— sand
— prime
— paint

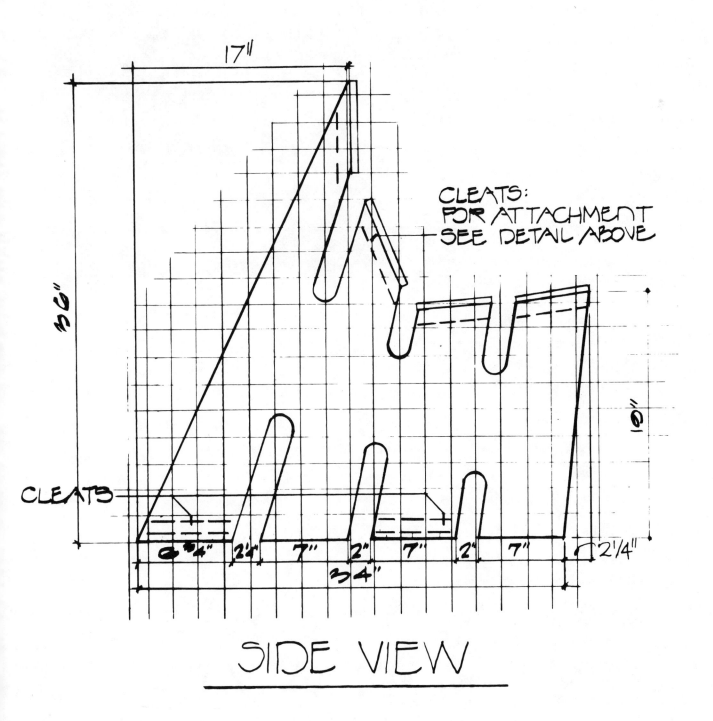

17"

36"

10"

CLEATS:
FOR ATTACHMENT
SEE DETAIL ABOVE

CLEATS

6¾" | 2" | 7" | 2" | 7" | 2" | 7" | 2¼"

34"

SIDE VIEW

5 LOUNGE BED

![Mary Howard reclining on the lounge bed made of foam cylinders]

MARY HOWARD

Materials
— **eight** yards of fabric, 40" wide, treated
   with Scotch Guard
— **nine** foam rubber cylinders, 8" diameter
   x 36" length
— thread to match fabric

Tools
— sewing machine
— scissors
— needle
— ruler
— fabric marker

Method
Examine illustrations
— take fabric, 40" x 24'; reduce length from
   24' to 19'2"; reduce width from 40" to 39"
— lay your large piece of fabric out
— measure 1½" down the length of fabric
   on both sides of length, to allow for seam
   allowance
— fold fabric along 1½" marks on each side
— stitch seam on each side
— fold fabric so that your fabric is now 9'7"
   length and 36" width, with hem
   exposed; the fabric is inside-out

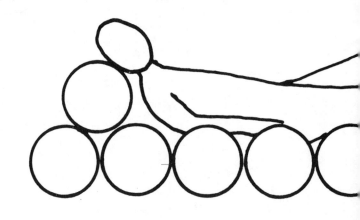

— measure in ½'' of both ends and sew
down seam so that both ends are sewn
together

— turn fabric outside-in

— you now have a wide sleeve for **eight**
cylinders; your fabric is now 36'' width
and 114'' length

— with right side out and starting at sewn
edge, begin measuring in 12½'' along
length of fabric, then 2'', then 12½'', and
so on across length of fabric

— use fabric marker to draw line down
width of fabric

— you will have **eight** sections 12½'' wide
and **seven** sections 2'' wide

— stitch along lines drawn

— fit each of the **eight** cylinders into their
respective **eight** sections; put aside

— from remaining fabric, cut out fabric 26'' x 39''

— as before, measure in 1½'' on both sides
of fabric (the 26'' sides)

— fold, sew

— measure ½'' on both ends; stitch to join
both ends

— turn fabric outside-in; you now have a
sleeve for your **ninth** cylinder

— with remaining fabric, make **eighteen**
circles for end caps; each circle has 12''
diameter

— cut out circles

— lay **one** circle over the end of each
cylinder, stuff in circumference of circle
under the cuff of each cylinder sleeve,
push in to fit end-circle smoothly over
each end

— sew end-circles in place along 1½'' seam

Optional

— use **two** different color fabrics, **one** color
for the section with **eight** cylinders and
another color for the section with the
ninth cylinder

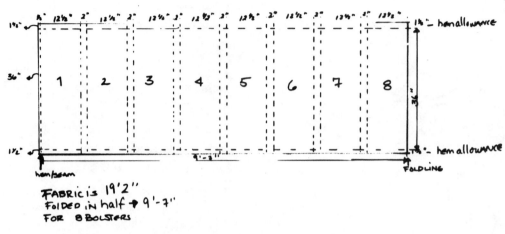

2" 12½" 2" 12½" 2" 12½" 2" 12½" 2" 12½" 2" 12½" 2" 12½" 1" 12½"

1½" — hem allowance

1½"

36"

| 1 | 2 | 3 | 4 | 5 | 6 | 7 | 8 |

36"

1½"

1½" — hem allowance

hem/seam

9'-3"

FOLDLINE

FABRIC is 19'2"
FOLDED in half → 9'-7"
FOR 8 BOLSTERS

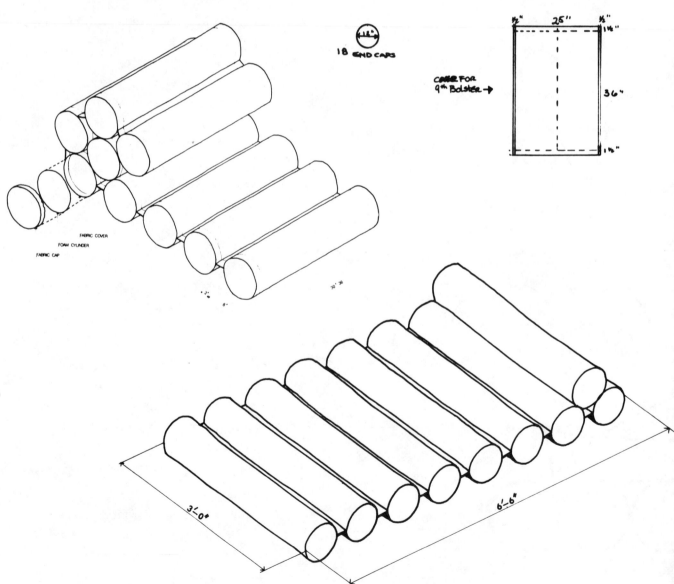

18 END CAPS

FABRIC COVER
FOAM CYLINDER
FABRIC CAP

½" 25" ½"
1½"

COVER FOR
9th BOLSTER →

36"

1½"

3'-0"

6'-6"

6 THE KNOCKDOWNABLE SENSUOUS TOPOGRAPH

STEPHANIE DIETERICH

Materials

— **four** pieces clear pine, each 5/4'' x 12'' x 49½''
— **one** piece clear pine, 5/4'' x 3'' x 14'
— **twenty** flathead wood screws, 2'' length
— white glue
— chalk to match fabric
— 3''-thick polyurethane
— fabric and thread for cushions (can be different colors)
— **four** upholstery zippers, 60'' each
— **one** 50' roll polyester fiber
— **three** pieces polyurethane, each 1'' x 2' x 3'
— 4'-square brown wrapping paper
— masking tape
— finishing nails, 2½''
— **eight** flathead screws, 2½
— **two** pieces plywood, each ¾'' x 2' x 4'
— pt. latex primer
— pt. latex paint

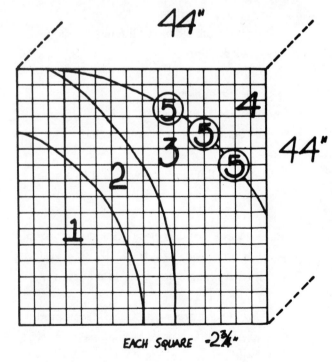

44"

44"

EACH SQUARE -2¾"

Tools

— belt sander
— table saw
— drill press
— screwdriver
— damp sponge
— C clamps
— paint brush
— pencil
— ruler
— scissors
— yardstick
— compass
— saw blade
— sewing machine

Method

Examine illustrations

— sand both sides of all **four** boards, using belt sander
— with table saw, cut tongue and groove as dimensioned
   sand— cut **four** 5/4'' x 3'' x 3' boards from the 5/4'' x 3'' x 14'; sand
— with drill press (the bit to accommodate the 2'' flathead screws), drill **five** holes in each length of 5/4'' x 3'' x 3' pine board
— from remaining clear pine, cut **two** small boards, each 5/4'' x 3'' x 9'', then split each piece lengthwise to measure 5/4'' x 1½'' x 9''
— with drill press and bit to accommodate 2'' flathead screws, drill holes in groove end of base boards
— assemble base, glue and screw the 5/4'' x 3'' x 3' boards with 2'' flathead screws to inside of **four** larger boards

(center them 7'' from top); let dry
— glue and nail (with 2½'' finishing nails) the 5/4'' x 1½'' x 9'' pieces in place, using ''C'' clamps; let dry
— fit tongue and groove joints together
— insert 2'' flathead screws
— place **two** pieces ¾'' x 2' x 4' plywood in base (to serve as support for cushions)
— prime
— paint

Cushions

— tape brown paper to make 4' square on work board
— draw grid, 2¾'' squares, **sixteen** squares to a side
— draw pattern on grid; circles are 6'' diameter (use compass)
— cut pattern pieces out (discard circles)
— calculate amount of 3'' thick polyurethane needed:

    3 layers for cushion #1 (9'' thickness)
    4 ''   ''   '' #2 (12'' '')
    6 ''   ''   '' #4 (18'' '')
    3 ''   ''   '' #3 (9'' '')

— cut polyurethane with saw blade or scissors to match pattern pieces for each cushion
— stack each set of polyurethane pieces and measure for side panels of cushions
— allow 2'' margin on all sides of fabric pieces
— allowing for cushions and three posts (4'' diameter x 2'2'' length) for coverings, calculate amounts of fabric needed; cut to size
— insert 60'' zippers in side panels, close to bottom (fig. 3)

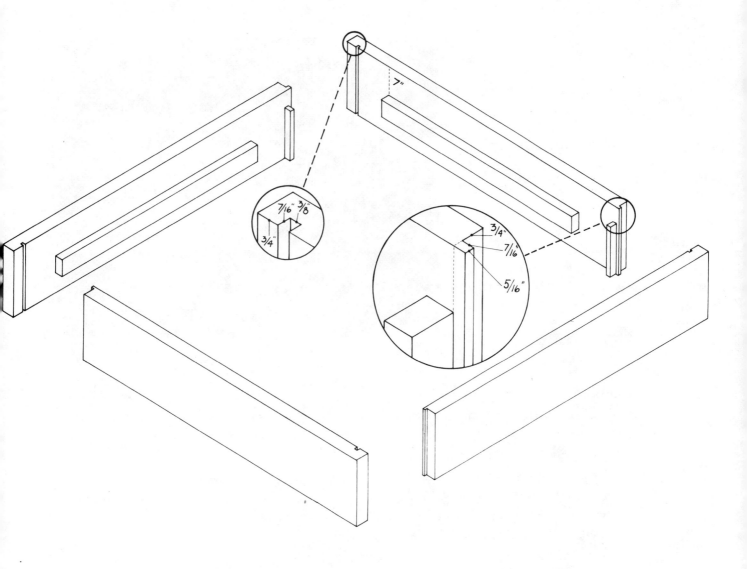

- sew top and bottom pieces to side panel; sew side panel closed; turn right side out
- sew cylindrical covers, leaving bottoms open
- wrap stacks #1, #2, #3, and #4 with polyester and stuff into cushions
- using **three** pieces 1″ x 2′ x 3′ polyurethane, roll 2″ edge as tightly as possible, wrap with polyester and stuff into cylindrical casings
- stitch bottom closed by hand
- arrange cushions and posts in frame

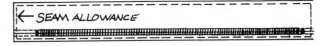

← SEAM ALLOWANCE

7 BANANA LOUNGE

STEPHANIE DIETERICH

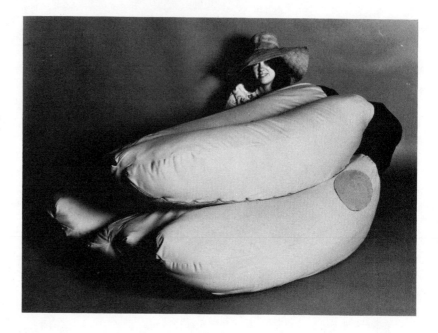

Materials

Note: Before purchasing foam and yellow
fabric, read **Method**

— **one** good-looking, curvy bunch of **five**
bananas, each with **four** skin panels
— **three** sheets polyurethane, 2½'' x 6' x 7'
— **five**-pound bag polyurethane scraps
— **12** yds. 60''-wide yellow fabric
(polyester and cotton)
— **five** yds. 60''-wide stretchy green fabric
— **five** 60'' upholstery zippers
— carpet thread
— threads to match fabric
— **one** roll polyester fiber, fifty ft. long
— ball of cord

Tools

— fine point felt-tip pen
— Exacto knife with #11 blade
— pencil
— graph paper
— brown wrapping paper, 20 yds.
— yardstick
— **one** piece light-colored chalk
— scissors
— sewing machine
— needles, sharps and darners
— toilet plunger

Method

Examine illustrations

— before separating bunch of bananas,
number each panel on each banana
with felt-tip pen as follows:

1st banana	1, 2, 3, 4
2nd ''	5, 6, 7, 8
3rd ''	9, 10, 11, 12
4th ''	13, 14, 15, 16
5th ''	17, 18, 19, 20

— make note of the position of each
banana in the bunch; you will be
duplicating each and assembling them

18

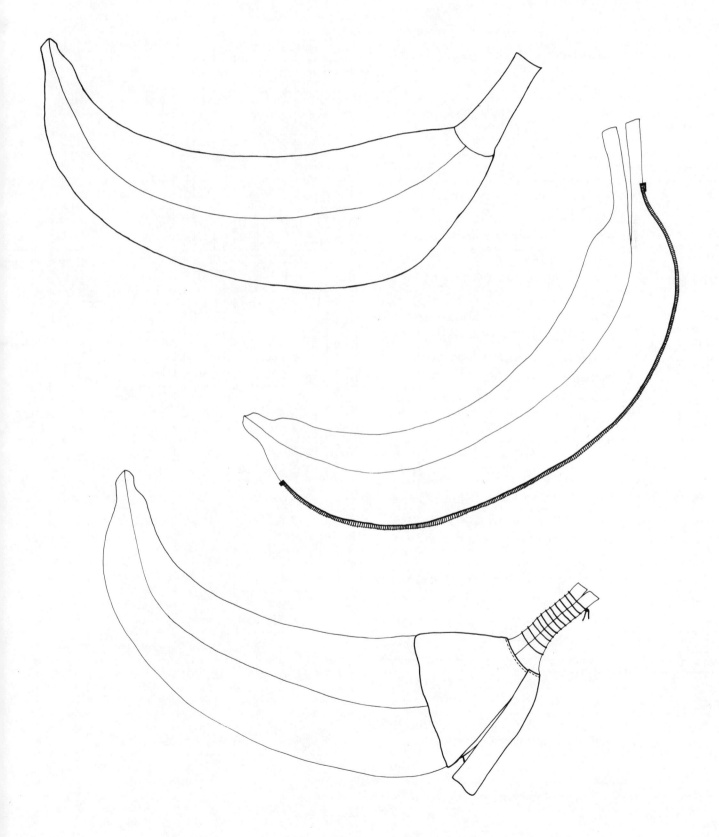

in the same order as the bunch before
you
— separate bananas
— draw a line around each banana (when
you split the skins off, the line will act
as a seam-matching guide, telling where
to attach one panel to another
— split skin at seams with Exacto knife and
remove skin
— place skin panels on graph paper; trace
outline in pencil, making sure to transfer
panel number and seam-matching guide
— on brown wrapping paper, enlarge the
graph to make each banana approximately **five** feet long; transfer banana-
skin outline, panel numbers, and
seam-matching guide
— repeat the above with **four** remaining
bananas
— cut out pattern pieces
— lay out all pattern pieces to confirm
amount of foam and fabric needed;
allow 2″ margin around pattern pieces
when cutting yellow fabric to accommodate polyester fiber and 2″ seam
allowance
— arrange pattern pieces on polyurethane
and mark outlines, panel numbers, and
seam-matching guides in chalk; cut
— place pattern pieces on fabric, allowing
2″ all around, to accommodate polyester
fiber and seam allowance; draw cutting
line on fabric
— in seam allowance, mark panel number
and seam-matching guide; cut

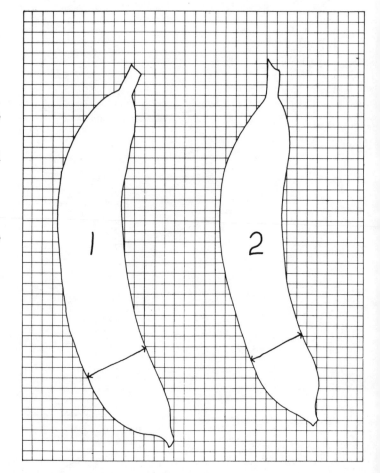

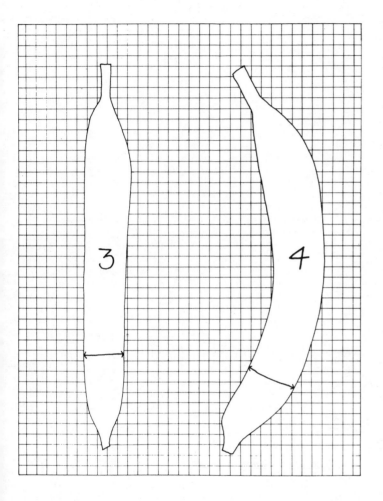

Method

— sew up yellow skins
— match up seam-matching guides, pin and sew **three** seams
— sew in zipper along a bottom seam of banana with zipper closing at wide part of banana shoulder (neck)
— sew other seams only up to wide part of shoulder, leaving necks open
— check bottom, make sure it is sewn closed
— task the **four** polyurethane panels iwth carpet thread up to wide part of neck, leaving top open for stuffing
— wrap a layer of polyester fiber around polyurethane shell, cutting excess folds away to shape it to form
— place bottom end of wrapped poly-urethane shell into bottom end of yellow banana-skin shell, making sure that the zipper will lie along proper seam
— slip banana skin up **one** or **two** ft. around polyurethane shell
— stuff scraps of polyurethane down into the cavity (made of banana-skin shell, polyester fiber, and polyurethane)
— use toilet plunger to stuff scraps into shell, making sure there are no empty pockets
— repeat last few instructions until banana is stuffed up to, but not including, narrow neck
— tie neck of banana together with cord
— sew around neck of banana a strip of green stretchy fabric, wide enough to go

around neck and 2' long

— pull green fabric up over stem and stitch
  the 2' seam

— place the bananas in same position as
  they were in the bunch

— tie the upper part of the necks together
  with cord

— stitch another piece of green fabric
  around collective necks, as you did for
  the singular necks; pull fabric up over
  necks, and stitch along seam

— stuff the stem cavity lightly with polyurethane scraps until the shape pleases
  you, and close up the opening

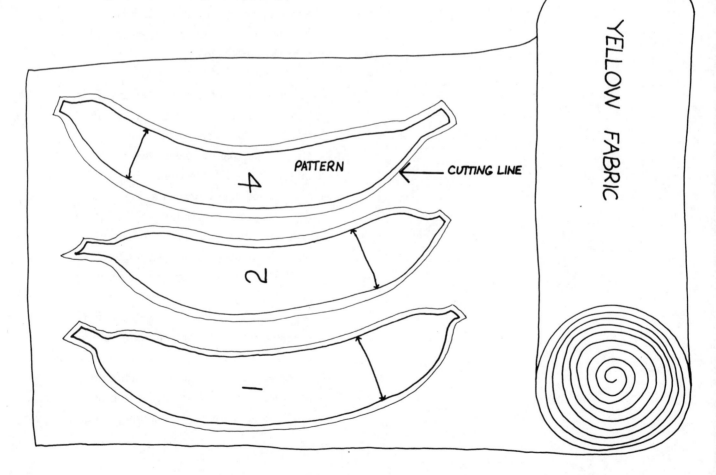

PATTERN

CUTTING LINE

4

2

1

YELLOW FABRIC

8 CHAIR

MELISSA TARDIFF

Materials

— **one** ¾" x 4' x 8' plywood, finished on
  one side
— **five** wooden dowels, 1" diameter:
  two 29" long and **three** 30¼" long
— **two** 2" long bolts, with washers and nuts
— **ten** 3" lag screws with washers
— **one** qt. paint
— **one** pt. shellac, cut 4 to 1 (thinner)
— **five** yds. 48" width fabric, canvas, or
  other sturdy fabric
— **one** roll polyester fiber, **fifty** yds. (see
  Cushion)
— fabric for cushion (see **Cushion**)
— fabric for cushion (see **Cushion**), 38" x
  134"
— thread to match fabric

Optional

— purchase ready-made cushion or make
  cushion to meaure 28" x 58"

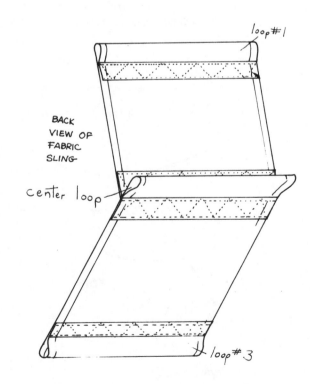

BACK
VIEW OF
FABRIC
SLING

loop #1

center loop

loop #3

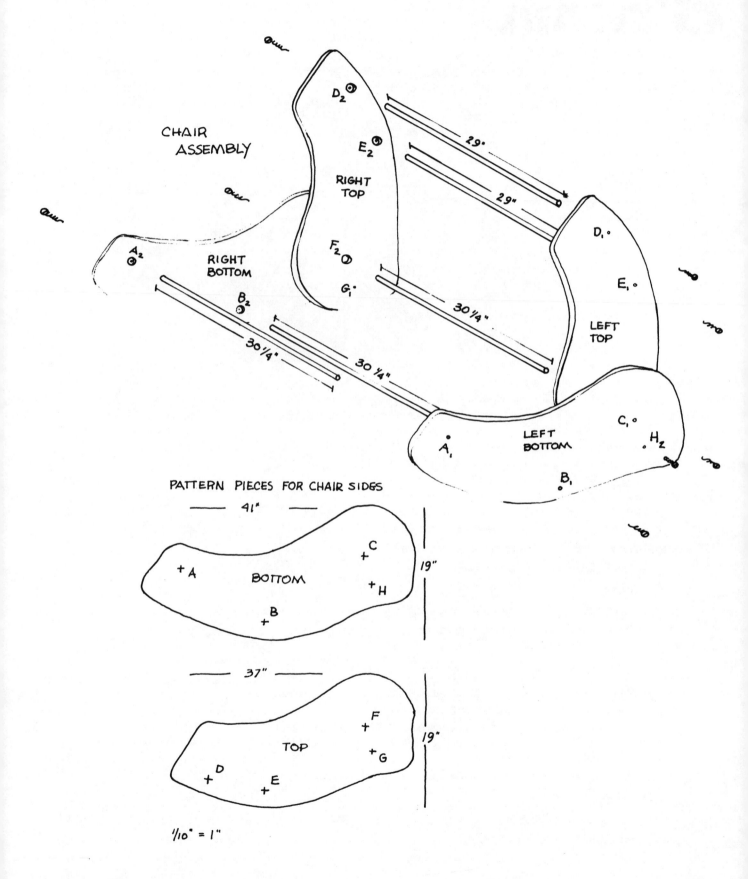

CHAIR ASSEMBLY

RIGHT TOP

RIGHT BOTTOM

D_2

E_2

F_2

G_1

A_2

B_2

29"

29"

30 1/4"

30 1/4"

30 1/4"

30 1/4"

D_1

E_1

LEFT TOP

C_1

A_1

B_1

LEFT BOTTOM

H_2

PATTERN PIECES FOR CHAIR SIDES

41"

19"

+ A

BOTTOM

+ C

+ H

+ B

37"

19"

TOP

+ F

+ G

+ D

+ E

1/10" = 1"

CUTTING LAYOUT FOR PLYWOOD

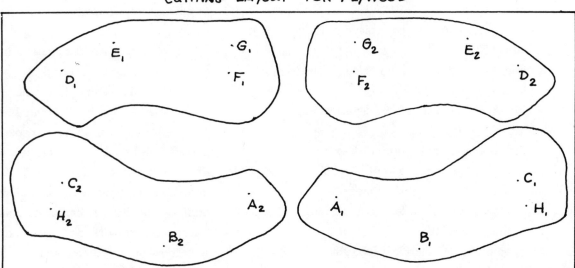

Tools

— jigsaw or bandsaw
— drill, 1"
— router
— screwdriver
— rasp
— sandpaper
— sewing machine
— scissors
— pins

Method

Examine illustrations

— lay out the **four** pattern pieces on plywood as shown
— cut out pieces with jigsaw or bandsaw
— transfer all markings to wrong side of plywood
— with 1" drill, countersink a hole 1/8" length into the wrong side of plywood at A, B, C, D, and E (left and right sides)

— using a bit to correspond to the size of the 3" length screw, drill completely through plywood in center of holes just countersunk
— with a 1"-diameter bit on router, drill completely through the plywood at F, left and right sides
— drill on outside of wood at holes A, B, C, D, and E (left and right sides) enough to countersink head of screw
— drill holes at G and H, both sides, completely through plywood, using bit to correspond with 2" long bolt
— drill holes into the ends of dowels, using 3/16" drill bit; size to accommodate the 3" long wood screws
— with rasp, round off edges of plywood
— sand smooth
— prime with **one** coat of shellac, cut 4 parts to 1

— paint
— for fabric sling, cut out a piece of fabric 30" x 67"
— fold under edges on long sides 1" and hem
— turn under short ends 5" and stitch across fabric 2½" from fold
— take another piece of fabric 15" x 30", hem 1" so piece measures 15" x 28"
— fold in half, so fabric now measures 7½" x 28" and stitch lengthwise down fabric 4" from the fold
— open out ends of fabric; place stitched seam across wrong side of sling on a line 29½" from a folded end, stitch flaps as shown
—to assemble chair, put **one** long dowel through the center back loop of fabric sling and the other long dowel through loop #3
— put a short dowel through remaining loop #1 of fabric sling
— put one end of center dowel through hole F, left side, and into the countersunk hole at C, left side
— insert wood screw into outside of holes C and F, left side, and into one end of center of dowel
— take short dowel at top of fabric sling and insert into countersunk hole at D, left side
— insert wood screw into outside of hole D and screw into end of dowel
— long dowel at bottom of fabric sling goes into hole A, left side, in like manner
— put remaining long dowel into hole B, left side, and remaining short dowel into hole E, left side, as above
— assemble free ends of **five** dowels into right side of chair in similar manner
— insert bolt and washer at holes G and H, securing with nut; do this to both sides of chair

Cushion (optional)
— fold 38" x 134" piece of fabric in half so it now measures 38" x 67"; make sure it is inside-out
— measure in 1" on all **three** open sides; mark off seam line on all **three** sides
— sew along seam line on **one** long side and on **one** short side
— now turn fabric right side out
— stuff with polyester fiber and sew up this last open side (long side); this last seam will be concealed by one side of the chair
— place cushion on fabric sling which is securely attached to chair frame

9 ROCKER

BILLY COHEN

Materials
— **one** sheet standard Masonite, ¼" x 4'10' x 2'8¾"
— **one** sheet standard Masonite, ¼" x 5'6½" x 2'8¾"
— **one** piece plywood, ¾" x 4' x 4'
— **five** pieces plywood, each 1" x 3" x 2'6"
— finishing nails, 1¼"
— Masonite nails, ¾" with heads
— white glue
— small tube plastic wood
— **one** qt. primer
— **one** qt. paint

Optional
— purchase cushion or make cushion to measure approximately 35" x 62"
— 3½ yds. of fabric, 48" wide (see Cushion)
— foam rubber, 3" thickness x 2'9" width x 5' length (see Cushion)
— **six** 1 lb. bags polyester fiber (see Cushion)
— thread (see Cushion)

Tools
— cardboard
  pencil
— saw
— hammer
— clamps
— sandpaper
— file
— plane
— 3" brush
— scissors (see Cushion)
— sewing machine (see Cushion)
— needle (see Cushion)

Method
Examine illustrations
— on cardboard, draw a semicircle with a diameter of 3'6"; the rim of semicircle is to measure 3" wide (this will serve as a template for the **six** semicircles needed for the plywood frame: A_1, A_2, A_3 and B_1, B_2, B_3)

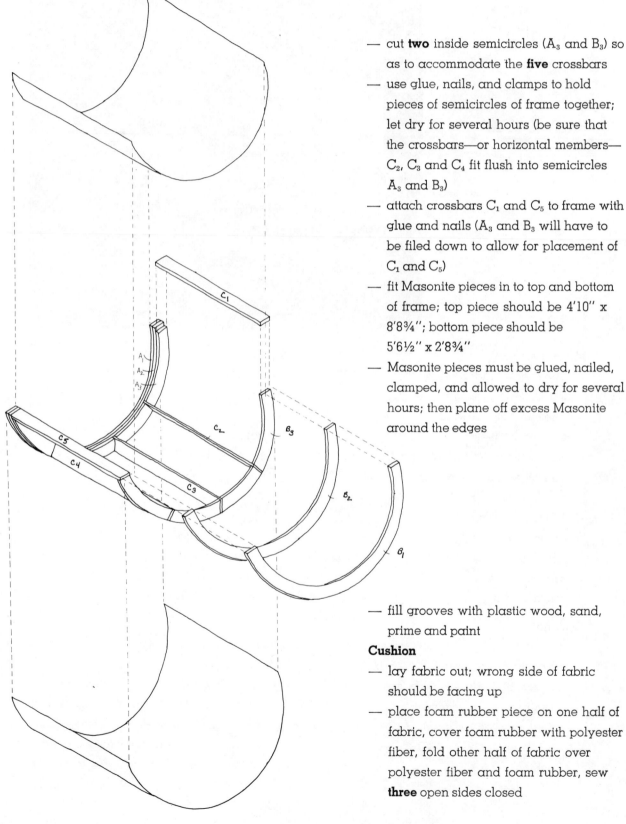

— cut **two** inside semicircles (A_3 and B_3) so as to accommodate the **five** crossbars

— use glue, nails, and clamps to hold pieces of semicircles of frame together; let dry for several hours (be sure that the crossbars—or horizontal members—C_2, C_3 and C_4 fit flush into semicircles A_3 and B_3)

— attach crossbars C_1 and C_5 to frame with glue and nails (A_3 and B_3 will have to be filed down to allow for placement of C_1 and C_5)

— fit Masonite pieces in to top and bottom of frame; top piece should be 4'10" x 8'8¾"; bottom piece should be 5'6½" x 2'8¾"

— Masonite pieces must be glued, nailed, clamped, and allowed to dry for several hours; then plane off excess Masonite around the edges

— fill grooves with plastic wood, sand, prime and paint

Cushion

— lay fabric out; wrong side of fabric should be facing up

— place foam rubber piece on one half of fabric, cover foam rubber with polyester fiber, fold other half of fabric over polyester fiber and foam rubber, sew **three** open sides closed

10 LOUNGE CHAIR

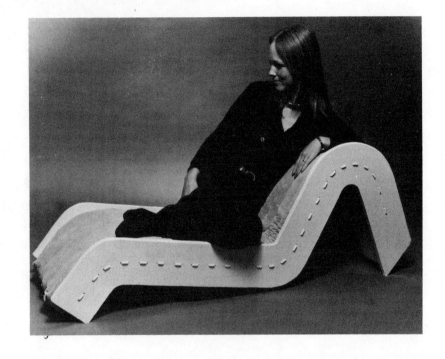

ASE ASK

Materials

— **one** piece plywood, ¾'' x 4' x 8'
  finishing nails, 1¼''
— finishing nails, 2''
— white glue
— clothesline, **ninety** ft.
— stain
— paint
— cotton velour fabric, 48'' wide x 8' long
  (see Cushion)
  seven 7 oz. bags of shredded foam filling
  (see Cushion)
— polyester roll, 1'' thickness (see Cushion)
— thread to match fabric

Optional

— purchase or make 1½' x 6' cushion

Tools

— pencil
— electric saw
— ruler
— sandpaper, fine and medium
— drill
— brush
— clamps, large furniture type
— scissors (see Cushion)
— needle (see Cushion)
— sewing machine (see Cushion)

Method

Examine illustrations

— make grid on plywood, using pencil;
  draw s-shaped pattern on plywood
— cut out **one** side panel and trace this
  exact form onto remaining plywood
— measure seat (18'' x 18'') and seat back
  (14'' x 18'') and cut out
— repeat above step; you will have two
  bottom seats (18'' x 18'') and two seat
  backs (14'' x 18'')
— finish all rough edges of **four** pieces of

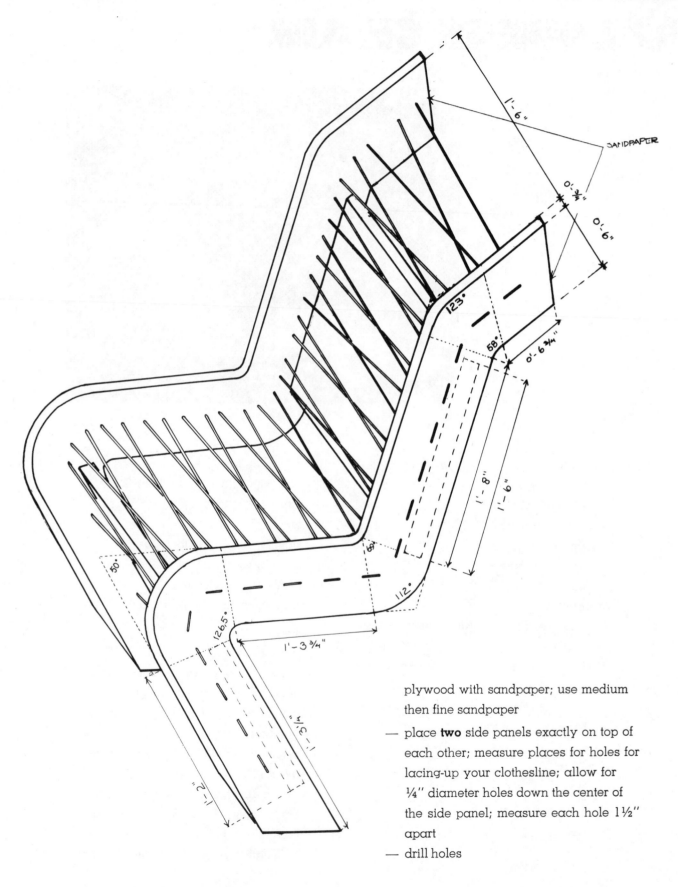

SANDPAPER

1'-6"

0'-¾"

0'-6"

123°

58°

0'-6¾"

1'-8"

1'-6"

59°

50

112°

126.5°

1'-3¾"

1'-3¾"

1'-2"

plywood with sandpaper; use medium
then fine sandpaper

— place **two** side panels exactly on top of
each other; measure places for holes for
lacing-up your clothesline; allow for
¼" diameter holes down the center of
the side panel; measure each hole 1½"
apart

— drill holes

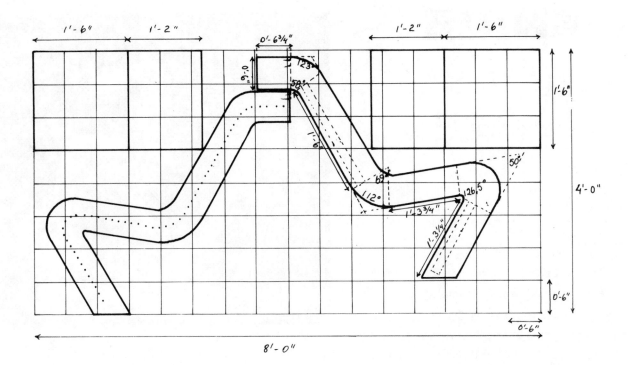

— take **two** seat back pieces of plywood (each 14″ x 18″) and glue together, one on top of the other (opposite grain direction for strength)

— reinforce gluing with 1¼″ nails, one in each corner

— clamp; let dry

— take **two** bottom seat pieces of plywood (each 18″ x 18″) and glue together, one on top of the other (opposite grain direction for strength)

— reinforce gluing with 1¼″ nails, one in each corner

— clamp; let dry

— glue and nail (2″ nails) seat back and bottom seat to **two** side panels; let dry, using large furniture clamps

— stain wood; let dry

— paint wood; let dry

— lace up chair with clothesline

— cushion chair

Cushion

— fold fabric so that the wrong side is showing and it measures over 1½′ x 6′ (to allow for stuffing)

— fold lengthwise

— sew **one** length closed and **one** width closed

— turn fabric right side out

— mark off widths (each pocket was 4¼″ wide) across top of open seam

— with pencil, draw lines from the open end of your fabric down the length of your fabric

— sew along these lines, forming equal-sized pockets down length of fabric

— stuff with shredded foam filling

— sew cushion closed

11 FREE-FORM GARDEN CHAIR

BILLY COHEN

Materials

— **one** sheet plywood, ¾" x 3' x 4'
— **one** dowel, 3" diameter x 6½' long
— 184 rivets for ⅜" holes
— white glue
— clothesline, 920" long
— **one** qt. primer
— **one** qt. paint

Tools

— sheet cardboard
— pencil
— electric jigsaw
— file
— sandpaper
— drill
— large clamps

Method

Examine illustrations

— enlarge grid on a sheet of cardboard so
  that each square in the grid is 2" x 2"
— on this grid, copy the outline of the two
  forms proportionately or improvise the
  forms a bit
— once patterns are drawn, cut them out,
  place them on the plywood, and trace
  around the edges
— be sure to mark the holes for the dowels

(crossbars) and clothesline correctly or
you may get a lopsided chair
— with electric jigsaw, cut out the forms
— use a file and sandpaper to smooth out
  any rough spots
— with a ⅜" drill bit, drill holes for the
  clothesline and rivets
— use a large drill bit to cut out holes for
  dowels; make the holes smaller than the
  dowel, about ¾" in diameter
— cut dowels into **four** pieces, 19½" long
— chisel off ¾" around the circumference
  at each end of all **four** dowels, to a
  length of ¾", so that each end of the
  dowels fits tightly into the plywood
  forms, and flush against their outside
— glue and then clamp the chair together
— let dry for several hours
— prime
— paint
— glue rivets into place; let dry
— lace up the chair

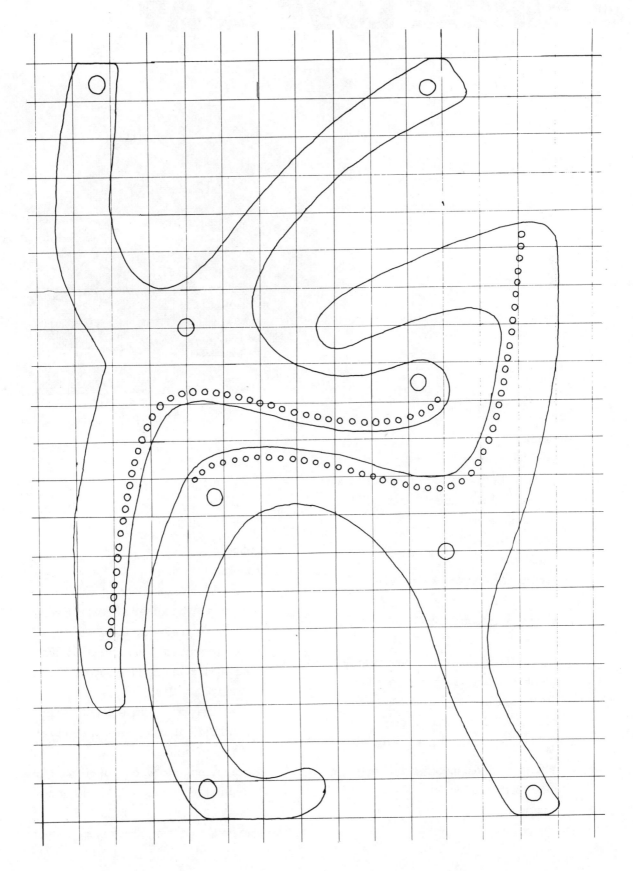

12 CIRCLE LOVE SEAT

BILLY COHEN

Materials

— **one** sheet plywood, ¾" x 4' x 8'
— **one** sheet standard Masonite, ⅛" x 4' x 8'
— **three** 1" x 3"s, each **ten** ft. long
— box of nails, ½"
— box of nails, 1½"
— white glue
— **six** yards fabric, 48" wide
— staples, 5/16"
— **one** piece of foam, 3" x 4' x 5'
— **one** piece of foam, 1" x 3' x 7'
— **four** to **six** one lb. bags of polyester fiber (relative to how much you wish to stuff the cushions)
— piping, ¼" diameter x 15' long

Tools

— soft pencil and 2 ft. long string, to use in place of a compass
— jigsaw
— compass

— hammer
— tape measure
— clamps
— staple gun

Method

Examine illustrations

— take ¾" x 4' x 8' plywood sheet, cut out a circle 4' in diameter (piece A), allowing the circle to overlap the edge of the wood so that a 3' long base (bottom edge) is created for the curved piece to stand on
— the center of the circle is point A and it is 1'3¾" above the bottom edge of your plywood sheet
— from remaining wood, cut out seat (piece B), front (pieces C and D), and arm pieces (pieces E_1, E_2, E_3, and E_4)
— to find the curve of front piece C, first cut

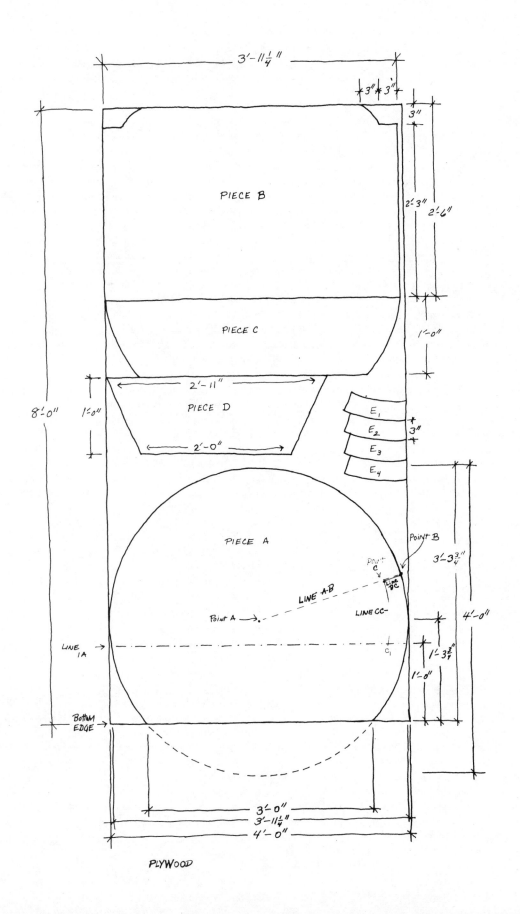

3'-11¼"

3" 3"

3"

PIECE B

2'-3" 2'-6"

PIECE C

1'-0"

8'-0" 1'-0" 2'-11"

PIECE D

2'-0"

E₁
E₂   3"
E₃
E₄

PIECE A

Point B

Point C

3'-3¾"

LINE A-B

Line DC

LINE CC-

Point A

4'-0"

C₁

LINE 1A

1'-3¾"

1'-0"

Bottom EDGE

3'-0"
3'-11¼"
4'-0"

PLYWOOD

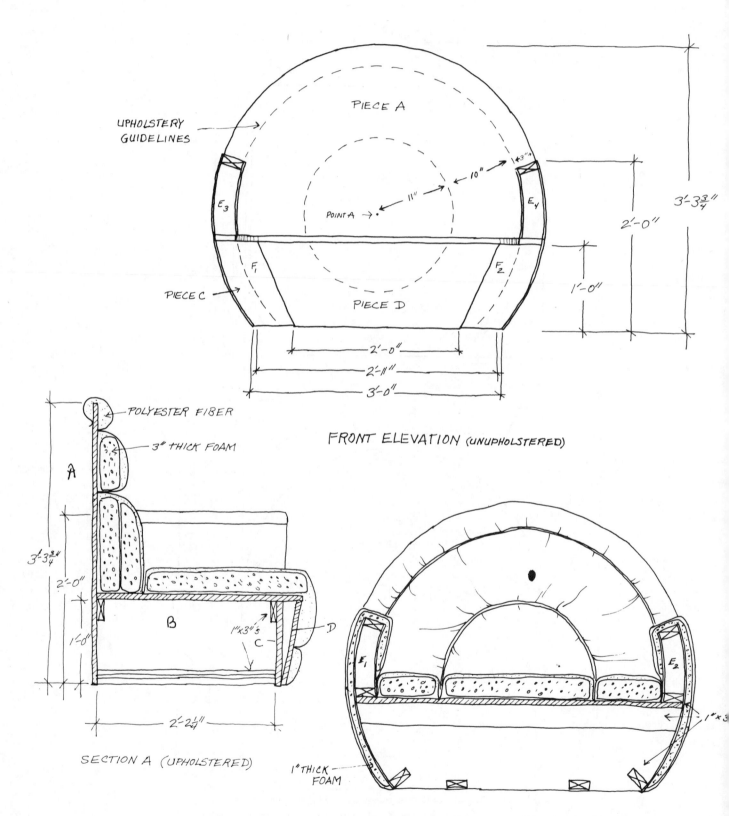

UPHOLSTERY GUIDELINES

PIECE A

POINT A →

11"

10"

3"

E_3

E_4

F_1

F_2

PIECE C

PIECE D

$3'-3\frac{3}{4}''$

$2'-0''$

$1'-0''$

$2'-0''$

$2'-11''$

$3'-0''$

FRONT ELEVATION (UNUPHOLSTERED)

POLYESTER FIBER

3" THICK FOAM

A

$3'-3\frac{3}{4}''$

$2'-0''$

$1'-0''$

B

D

C

$1''\times3''$s

$2'-2\frac{1}{4}''$

SECTION A (UPHOLSTERED)

E_1

E_2

$1''\times3$

1" THICK FOAM

SECTION B (UPHOLSTERED)

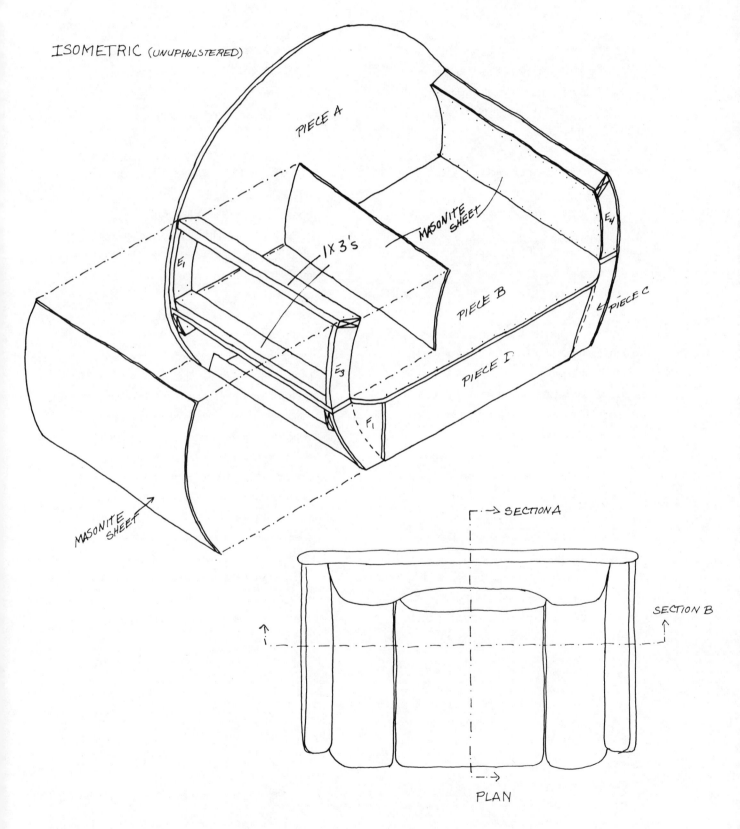

ISOMETRIC (UNUPHOLSTERED)

PIECE A

MASONITE SHEET

E_4

1X3's

PIECE B

PIECE C

E_1

PIECE D

E_3

F_1

MASONITE SHEET

→ SECTION A

SECTION B

PLAN

37

out a rectangle 1' x 4'; place this piece under piece A, between "bottom edge" and line 1A, then simply trace the curve (you'll have to cut out piece A before doing this step)

— to make E_1, E_2, E_3, and E_4, measure up 11" from line 1A on piece A; mark this point B

— draw a broken line connecting point B with point A; call this line AB

— starting at point B on line AB, measure in 3"; call this point C

— connect point C to point B; line BC will define the top of the arm

— use a compass, starting at point A, to measure off line CC; this is the shape for all four E pieces

— to make E pieces, cut out a pattern of this shape on paper and trace it four times onto the plywood

— glue and nail (use ½" nails) pieces A, B, C, and D together

— reinforce with 1" x 3"s wherever they are indicated in illustrations

— glue and nail pieces E_1 and E_2 onto piece A, then glue and (1½" nails) nail 1" x 3"s and finally pieces E_3 and E_4

— with a tape measure, measure outsides and insides of arms in order to obtain correct size of Masonite pieces

— cut out Masonite pieces; glue, nail, and clamp; allow to dry overnight

To Upholster

— on wood, measure off upholstery guidelines

— staple fabric over foam and polyester fiber along these guidelines

— cut 3"-thick foam to the shapes of the open spaces F_1 and F_2 so that the front of the loveseat will take correct shape; glue in place onto wood

— cut out 1"-thick foam pieces to fit sides and arm rests

— place foam onto Masonite sides with white glue

— cover this with fabric and staple onto Masonite

Note: Use upholstery guidelines to help you estimate size of pieces of fabric needed to cover each section of the chair, remembering each section will be stuffed with 3"-thick foam and polyester fiber, and be sure to allow for enough fabric around the edges which you will need to staple to wood (broken lines represent upholstery guidelines).

If you desire, the **three** sections of your back rest may be stuffed with different amounts of foam and polyester (see illustration).

13 WOOD STOOL

THOMAS CLOUGH

Materials
— **one** piece plywood, ¾'' x 8'' x 21'', preferably with oak veneer, for seat
— **one** roll wood tape, approximately 1'' wide
— **one** piece white oak, 2¾'' x 2¾'' x 21'', for pedestal base
— **one** piece white oak, 1½'' x 2¾'' x 20½'', for T-support
— **one** piece white oak, 2'' x 2¾'' x 22'' for pedestal
— **one** piece white oak, 2'' x 2'' x 14'', for seat support
— **two** pieces white oak, ⅞'' x 2'' x 15'', for seat support
— casein white glue
— **one** bolt, ⅜'' diameter x 3¾'' long, with round or hex head
— **one** washer and hex nut for above
— **eighteen** 1½'' ten gauge cadmium plated iron wood screws
— **one** iron strap, 3/32'' x 1'' x 5½''
— **one** iron bolt, 5/16'' diameter x 1'' long, with flat head
— **one** square nut for above
— **one** sheet white railroad board, 22'' x 28'' (from art store)

Tools
— pencil
— screwdriver
— wrench
— mallet and chisel
— saber saw
— block plane
— sandpaper
— crosscut saw and miter box or electric circular saw

— hammer
— drill
— square
— hacksaw blade
— single-edged razor blade

Method

Note: Two alternative stool assemblies are illustrated. One is simpler and more monolithic but requires the laborious process of cutting a mortise and tenon joint in solid oak. The alternative construction, only suggested here, produces the same form from the same material, but necessitates a more involved gluing and clamping operation and the use of additional bolts or screws; the making of the mortise and tenon, however, is reduced to simple miter crosscuts.

The Seat: The table and its accompanying diagram can be used to create a full-size template for cutting out the plywood seat. Simply draw a fine horizontal line down the length of your piece of railroad board (the line should be centered on your board). On this horizontal reference line erect **thirteen** perpendiculars ¼" apart. Leave a 10" gap to the right of these lines and then draw **twenty-nine** more perpendiculars also ¼" apart. Leave a 10" gap to the right of these lines and then draw **twenty-nine** more perpendiculars also ¼" apart.

If the lines are numbered as in the diagram with line zero on the extreme left, then merely by placing a pencil dot on each line in correspondence with the values listed in the table and connecting dots, it is possible to make a facsimile of half the stool seat.

Cut out the pattern.

Draw a light line down the center of your plywood (parallel to the grain). Lay the reference line of your seat pattern along this line. Draw around the pattern. Now flip your pattern over to draw the other half of the seat.

Cut the seat out with a saber saw fitted with a hacksaw blade; the fine teeth cause less "ragging" of the plywood edge.

Seat support: As shown in the exploded view, **three** pieces of oak are joined with screws and glued to form the seat support. They must be cut so as to sit snugly against the pedestal. The middle piece is mitered so that its butt end sets flat against the pedestal face.

Seat journey: See detail drawing "Seat Support Assembly." The iron strap is first drilled to accommodate the bolt and to allow the countersinking of screws; it is then bent. Some of the plywood must be chiseled away from the underside of the seat in order to recess the strap. A bolt secures the strap to the seat. A hole in the pedestal top accommodates the nut. The transverse hole allows passage of the bolt which secures the seat support assembly to the pedestal

Mortise and tenon: The mortise and tenon are 1⅛" wide. The joint is glued.

Finishing touches: When the stool is completely assembled, sand the seat edge and dress it with wood tape. Wood tape is a very thin strip of real wood; it is 1" wide and comes in 8' lengths. Simply glue it over the exposed end-grain wtih white glue and trim off the excess with a single-edged razor blade.

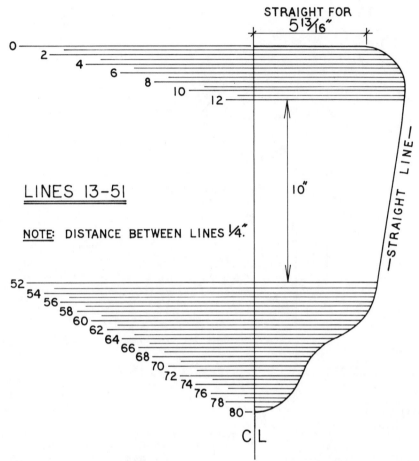

LINES 13-51

NOTE: DISTANCE BETWEEN LINES ¼."

STRAIGHT FOR 5 13/16"

10"

STRAIGHT LINE

C L

LINE	DISTANCE FROM C.L. TO CURVE	LINE	DISTANCE FROM C.L. TO CURVE
1	6 13/16	60	5 25/32
2	7 7/32	61	5 ½
3	7 31/64	62	5 11/64
4	7 43/64	63	4 45/64
5	7 53/64	64	4 7/32
6	7 61/64	65	3 51/64
7	8 1/32	66	3 37/64
8	8 5/64	67	3 15/64
9	8 1/8	68	3 1/64
10	8 3/32	69	2 27/32
11	8 5/64	70	2 47/64
12	8 7/64	71	2 5/8
52	6 5/8	72	2 33/64
53	6 37/64	73	2 27/64
54	6 35/64	74	2 7/16
55	6 ½	75	2 5/32
56	6 27/64	76	1 31/32
57	6 5/16	77	1 47/64
58	6 11/64	78	1 29/64
59	6	79	1 7/64

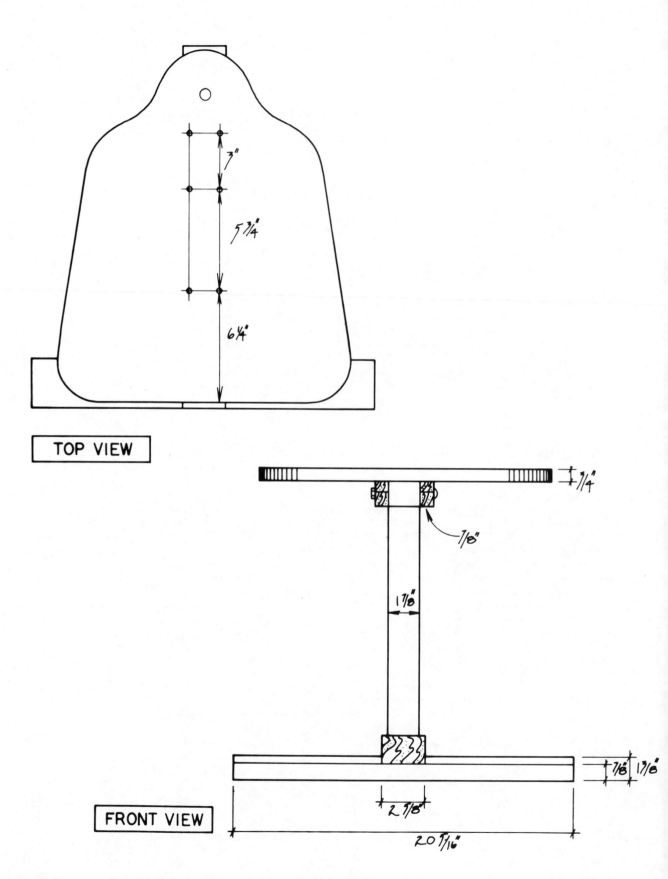

TOP VIEW

FRONT VIEW

3"

5 3/4"

6 1/4"

3/4"

1/8"

1 7/8"

7/8" 1 3/8"

2 5/8"

20 5/16"

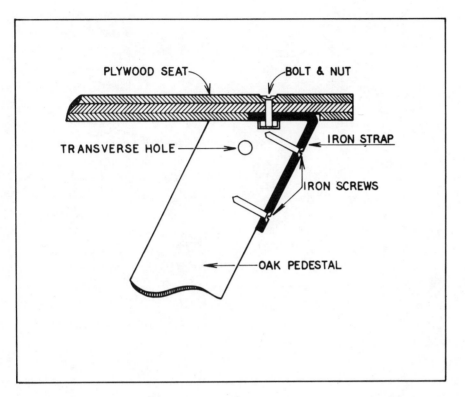

PLYWOOD SEAT

BOLT & NUT

TRANSVERSE HOLE

IRON STRAP

IRON SCREWS

OAK PEDESTAL

DETAIL

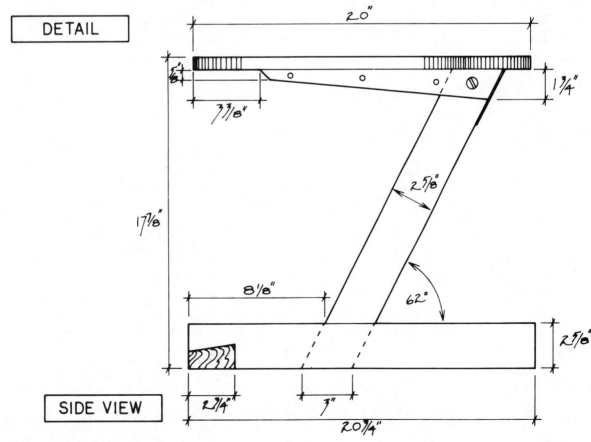

20"

1 3/4"

3 3/8"

2 5/8"

17 7/8"

8 1/8"

62°

2 5/8"

2 3/4"

3"

20 1/4"

SIDE VIEW

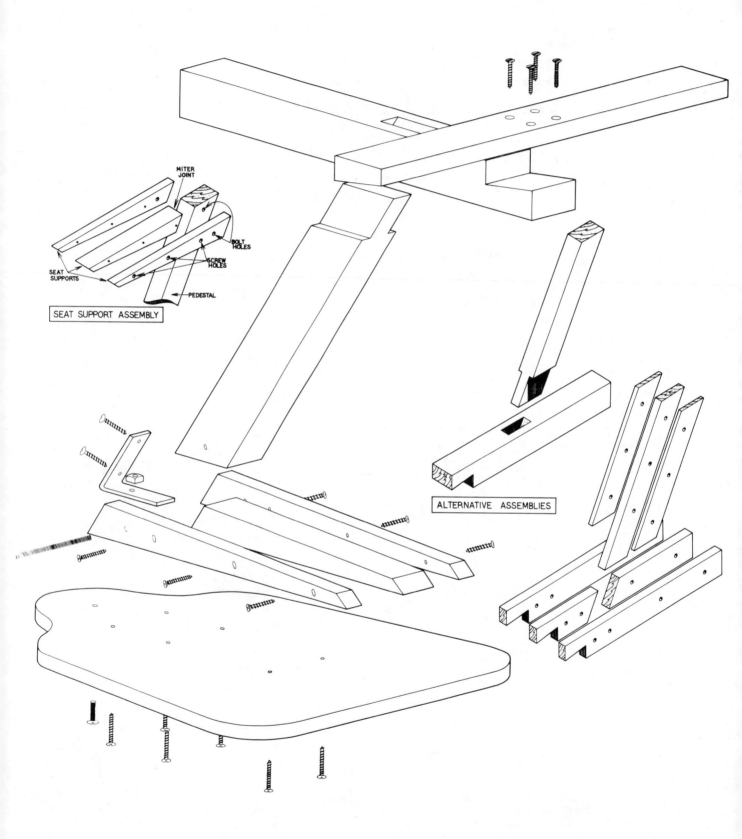

MITER JOINT

SEAT SUPPORTS

BOLT HOLES

SCREW HOLES

PEDESTAL

SEAT SUPPORT ASSEMBLY

ALTERNATIVE ASSEMBLIES

4 PLYWOOD CHAIR

MARTIN SPIEGEL

Materials

— **two** sheets plywood, ¾'' x 4' x 8' (interior grade; good on one side)
— **two** pieces pine board, 1'' x 3'' x 8'
— **one** small container Quik glue (Slomon's Labs)
— **one** small box finishing nails, 1¼'' (17 gauge)
— **one** package coarse sandpaper
— **one** package medium sandpaper
— **one** medium-size can plastic wood

Optional

— high gloss enamel paint (**six** coats)
— polyurethane sealer

Tools

— saw
— hammer
— power sander
— ruler or tape measure
— pencil
— square
— putty knife
— **two** clamps (adjustable)

Optional

— **two** paint brushes
— **one** package sandpaper (fine grade)

Method

Examine illustrations

— from **two** sheets plywood, ¾'' x 4' x 8', cut the following pieces with a saw:

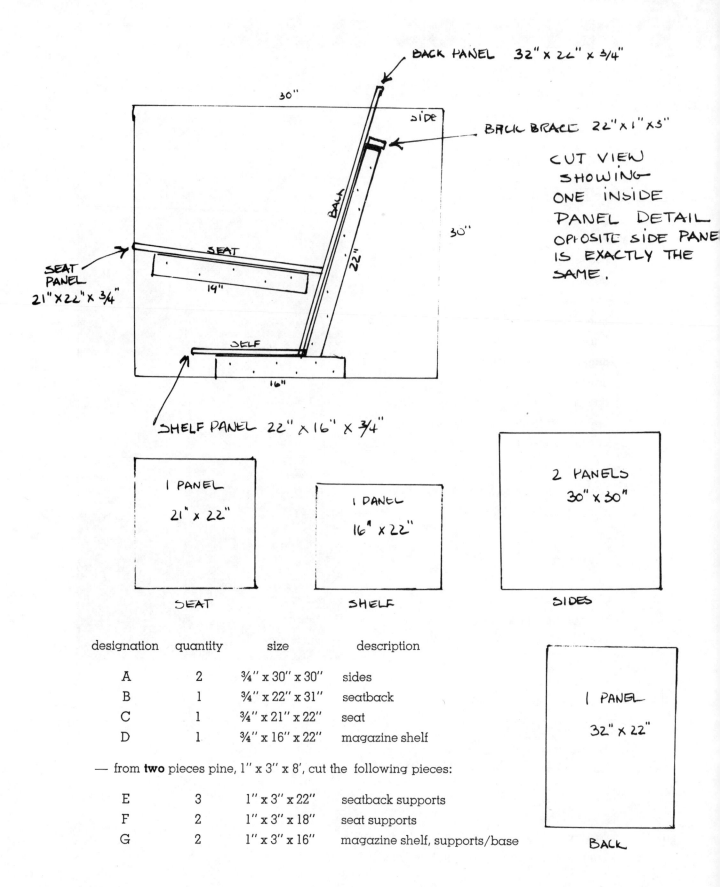

BACK PANEL 32" x 22" x 3/4"

SIDE

BACK BRACE 22" x 1" x 3"

CUT VIEW
SHOWING
ONE INSIDE
PANEL DETAIL
OPPOSITE SIDE PANEL
IS EXACTLY THE
SAME.

30"

30"

BACK

22"

SEAT

SEAT
PANEL
21" x 22" x 3/4"

14"

SHELF

16"

SHELF PANEL 22" x 16" x 3/4"

1 PANEL

21" x 22"

SEAT

1 PANEL

16" x 22"

SHELF

2 PANELS
30" x 30"

SIDES

1 PANEL

32" x 22"

BACK

designation	quantity	size	description
A	2	¾" x 30" x 30"	sides
B	1	¾" x 22" x 31"	seatback
C	1	¾" x 21" x 22"	seat
D	1	¾" x 16" x 22"	magazine shelf

— from **two** pieces pine, 1" x 3" x 8', cut the following pieces:

E	3	1" x 3" x 22"	seatback supports
F	2	1" x 3" x 18"	seat supports
G	2	1" x 3" x 16"	magazine shelf, supports/base

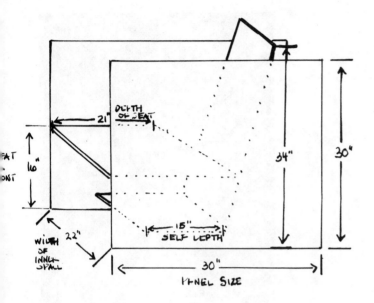

DEPTH OF SEAT

21"

16"

SEAT FRONT

34"

30"

15"
SEAT DEPTH

22"

WIDTH OF INNER SPACE

30"
PANEL SIZE

— after cutting out the pieces put them together as follows:
— take the A pieces and separate them to form **two** piles
— in each pile place **one** E, F, and G piece
— now using a ruler or tape measure lay out pieces E, F, G on piece A as it is done in the diagram
— after both A pieces are laid out this way and measured, the E, F and G pieces should be glued down
— before the glue dries, about **ten** nails should be hammered in
— make sure that right side and left side pieces match and are opposite
— stand both A pieces up and insert B, C and D pieces in the following manner:

    D should rest on the lower lip (or on top edge of G) with some glue and nails

    B should be slipped in with glue and nailed to front lip on E

— finally C should be put in place with some glue and then nailed to upper lip of F (after it is pushed as tightly together with E)
— the last piece, the remaining E, should span from top of E right side to top of E left side; glue and nail
— the final details of paint or stain and cushions are left to the taste of the builder

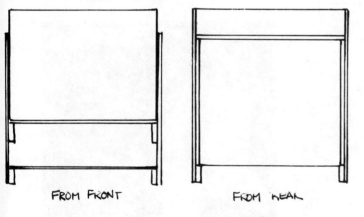

FROM FRONT   FROM REAR

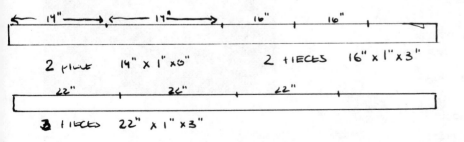

14"   17"   16"   16"

2 PIECE   14" x 1" x 3"   2 PIECES   16" x 1" x 3"

22"   22"   22"

3 PIECES   22" x 1" x 3"

15 U-TURN CHAIR

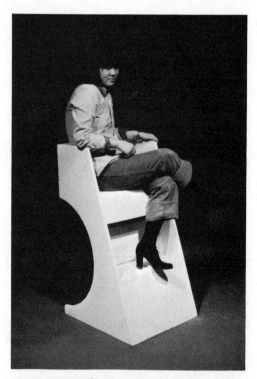

YUTAKA MATSUMOTO

Materials
— plywood, ¾'' x 4' x 7'
— **six** dozen finishing nails, 2''
— white glue
— sandpaper #120
— **one** pt. white paint

Tools
— electric jigsaw
— hammer
— wood clamp
— compass
— brush

Method
Examine illustrations
— drawing No. 1 shows how to lay out
  your pieces
— draw the pieces on the plywood and cut
  pieces as shown, using an electric
  jigsaw
— assemble the pieces step by step,
  starting with No. 1, using white glue,
  hammer and nails and a wood clamp
  for stronger joints
— allow structure **one** hour to dry
— sand the rough joints and paint

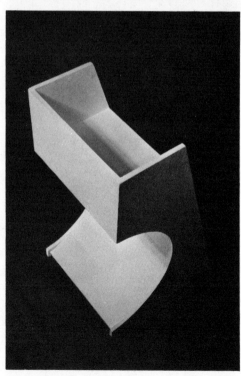

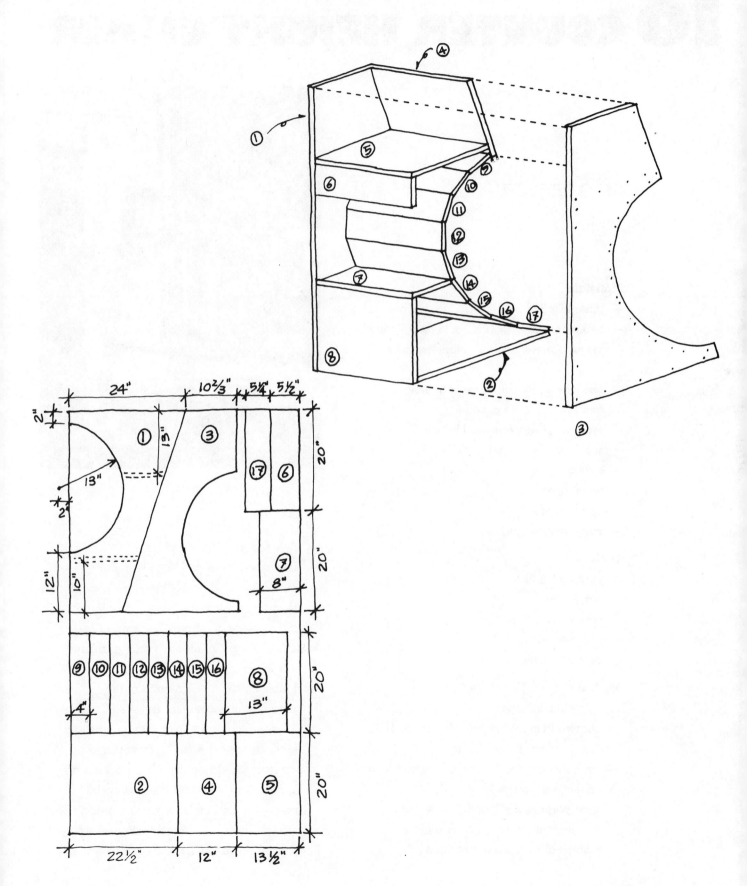

16 COUNTER HEIGHT CHAIR

GREG PETERSEN

Materials

— pine, 1" x 3" x 20'
— **two** strips pine, each ¾" x ½" x 10" long
— **seven** dowels, each 1" diameter x 19½" long
— **one** dowel, ¼" diameter x 5" long
— **four** ft. canvas, 1 yd. wide
— **ten** roundhead screws, 1⅛" long; washers
— strong thread
— wood glue
— sandpaper
— satin gloss varathane

Tools

— standard drill
— saber saw
— screwdriver
— drill bits, ¼" and 1"
— sewing needle

Method

Examine illustrations

— cut **two** identical pieces of parts A, B, C, and D and drill the 1" holes
— the holes marked F may vary depending on desired footrest level
— glue parts A, B, C, and D together making sure to keep joints tight; if clamps are available use them

— after pieces have dried, drill ¼" holes as marked (approx. 2⅝" deep)
— insert glue and dowels (dowels should be cut to approx. the depth of the hole)
— take a piece of canvas, approx. 18" x 18", overlap ½" on each side and sew it down to avoid ragged ends
— double-sew a loop on each of the remaining sides so that dowels G and H will fit in leaving 12" of canvas between them, center to center (at this point all sanding should be completed, including A, B, C, and D and all the 1" dowels)
— insert dowels in seat loops just made
— glue and insert 1" dowels into **one** side of the chair so that the ends of the dowels

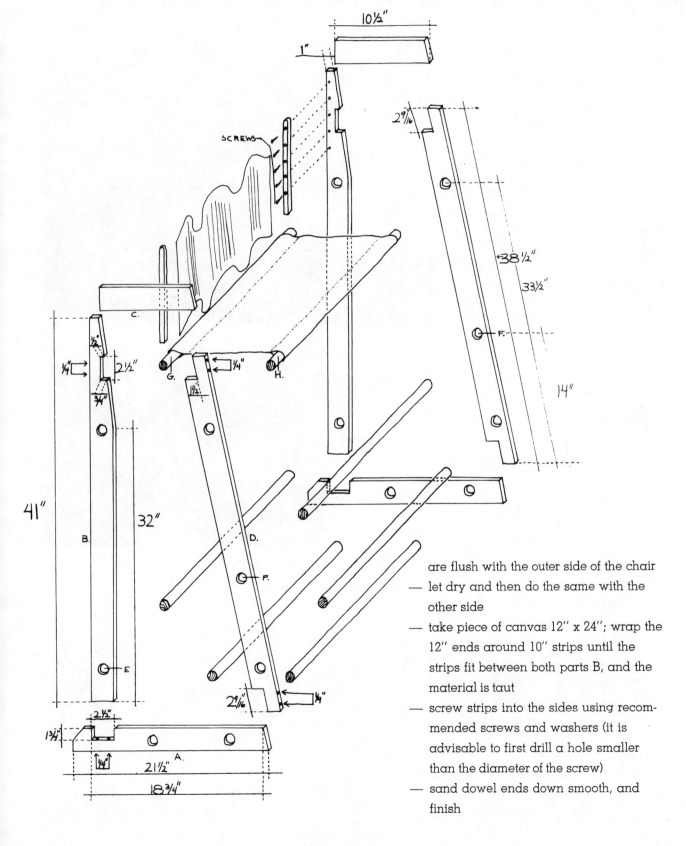

are flush with the outer side of the chair
— let dry and then do the same with the
other side
— take piece of canvas 12″ x 24″; wrap the
12″ ends around 10″ strips until the
strips fit between both parts B, and the
material is taut
— screw strips into the sides using recommended screws and washers (it is
advisable to first drill a hole smaller
than the diameter of the screw)
— sand dowel ends down smooth, and
finish

17 OUTDOOR TWO SEATER

SUSAN ORSINI

Materials
— **eight** pieces clear fir, 2½" x 2½" x 48"
— **three** pieces clear fir, 2½" x 2½" x 32"
— **one** piece clear fir, 2½" x 2½" x 22"
— **one** piece aluminum stripping, ⅛" x
   ¾" x 3' long
— **two** pieces aluminum stripping, ⅛" x
   ¾" x 8' long
— **one** piece nylon blend fishing net,
   48" x 48"; ¼" x 1¾" gauge
— **one** piece nylon blend fishing net,
   10" x 100"; ¼" x 1¾" gauge
— **one hundred** screws (aluminum), 1" long
   (number 7)
— **one** large container white glue
— box of tacks

Cushion (one cushion: 3½" x 48" x 48")
             (two cushions: 3½" x 10" x 48"
             each)
— **fourteen** lbs. shredded polyfoam

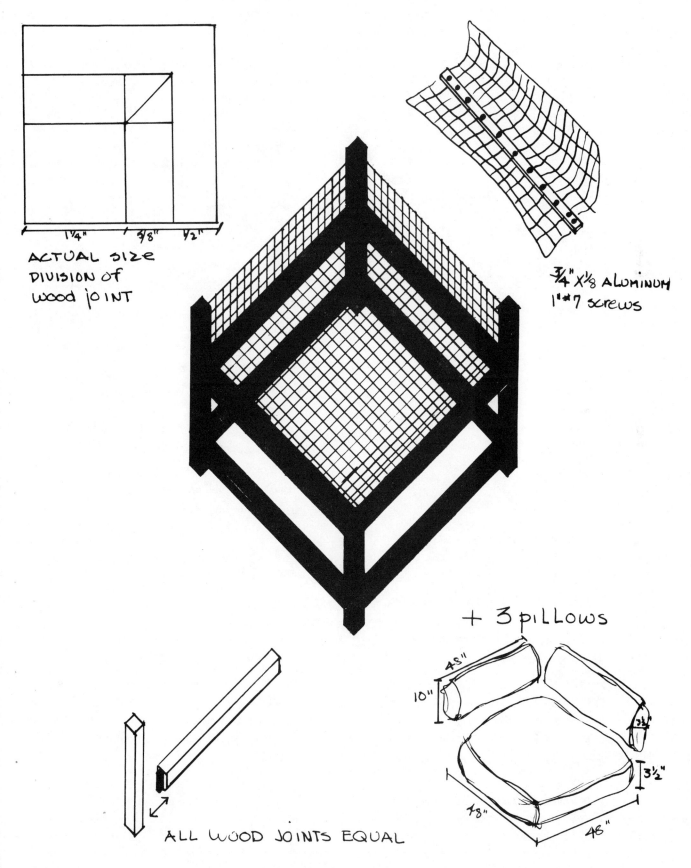

ACTUAL SIZE
DIVISION OF
WOOD JOINT

1¼" ⅜" ½"

¾" X ⅛ ALUMINUM
1" #7 screws

+ 3 pillows

48"
10"
3½"
3½"
48"
48"

ALL WOOD JOINTS EQUAL

— fabric, 56" x 157"
— **one** zipper 48" long
— **two** zippers, each 10" long
— **one** can wood sealer

Optional
— stain or paint

Tools
— pointer
— pencil
— drill press
— table saw
— mill file
— electric sander
— sandpaper
— clamps
— hand drill
— hacksaw
— screwdriver
— hammer
— scissors
— sewing machine

Method
Examine illustrations
— sand all wood
— determine facing sides of all pieces of wood; mark accordingly where joints will go
— working with 2½" x 2½" x 32" wood, use drill press with ½" bit
— cut 2½" x ¾" x 1" deep where marked according to joint dimension 3" x 19¾" from base (receiving end)
— to form projected section, cut on table saw an end with same dimension as receiver
— follow same procedure as above using

2½" x 2½" x 22" wood, except leave ½" shoulder at top
— cut groove ¾" x ¼" in top 10" of three taller legs and top inside ¾" of top supporting beams
— use mill file to round off edges of projected end
— use electric sander on all inner sides of wood
— sandpaper over all wood by hand (fir tends to have splinters)
— glue and clamp overnight two opposite ends
— clamp entire structure
— cut aluminum stripping to accommodate size of groove in wood:
    four pieces 42¾" long
    three pieces 10⅝" long
— use a hand drill and counter sink to locate screws 3½" on center along metal
— stain or paint frame (optional)
— stretch 48" x 48" net over bottom of frame, glue and tack
— place metal over, flush to edge, and screw in screws
— stretch 10" x 100" net over back; tack, glue and apply metal in the same way

Cushions
— sew cushion for seat very loosely to fit chair (3½" x 48" x 48")
— sew **three** sides first, then fill with poly-foam (approximately 9 lbs.)
— then sew **two** cushions (each 3½" x 10" x 48") on **three** sides and fill each with 2½ lbs. of polyfoam
— sew a zipper into each open end of each cushion

TABLES

There are different types of tables—dining, coffee, cocktail, side, night, tea, and so forth. Whatever it is called, the table should perform the service for which it is needed. In other words, obtain the height and size that best works for your needs. If, for example, you desire a surface for lighting next to a chair for reading, figure out the height you need to read comfortably. This can be done by stacking books and magazines up to the appropriate height.

Tables are probably the easiest kind of furniture to make because all you need is a flat top surface and a support for it. Of course, there are many ways of achieving this, and the spectrum of choices goes from glass to plastic pipes, to plywood, or even to heavy mat cardboard.

Magazines, ash trays, coffee, tea, cocktails, look out—here we come!

ORIGAMI TABLE

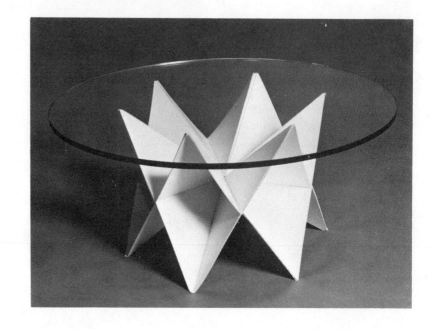

YUCHI

Materials
— **three** sheets of mat board
— glass, ½'' thick x 2'6'' diameter

Tools
— pencil
— ruler
— Exacto knife
— white glue
— steel straight edge

Method
Examine illustrations
— draw on the mat boards the folding lines,
  using a steel straight edge (T square)
  and knife as shown in the drawing;
  a line and a dotted line show the
  different cutting surface (one from the
  front and the other from the back)
— press both horizontal edges to make the
  center back
— fold and put glue on one small
  triangular part, one each side, then
  attach to the big triangular part
— fold to complete base
— place glass top on base

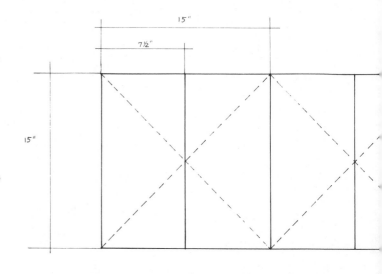

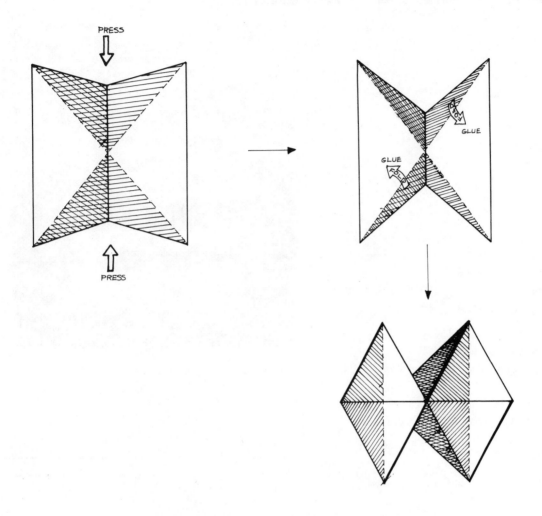

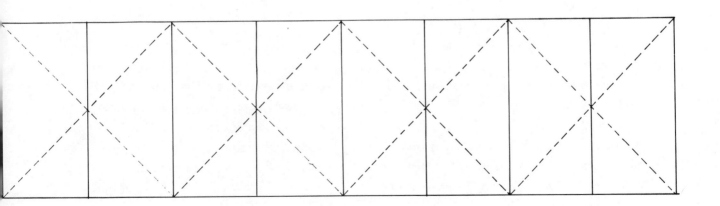

2 COFFEE TABLE

DEBBIE GOLD

Materials

— **four** pieces white pine, 16″ x 3″
— **eight** pieces white pine, 24″ x 3″
— 3½ yds. Ultra-suede, 45″ wide
— **four** wood vises with a 38″ bar

Tools

— 3 M Spray Mount for applying Ultra-suede to wood
— staple gun
— electric saw

Method

See illustrations

— place **four** 24″ x 3″ pieces of wood corner to form a square
— insert the **four** pieces of 16″ x 3″ wood with epoxy on the ends at corners, to form the legs
— place vises on opposite corners and hold in place for 12 hours
— turn table upside down and place the **four** remaining 24″ x 3″ pieces of wood in between the vertical 16″ x 3″ pieces of wood (glue is also applied to ends of longer wood)
— hold in place for 12 hours with wood vises

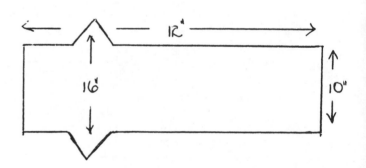

— after assembling table, cut a ¼″ x ¼″ groove along inside top rim of table using electric saw (see diagram)
— insert plexiglass
— to cut Ultra-suede, see diagram
— attach Ultra-suede to table using Spray Mount
— staple gun may be used to reinforce suede at corners

58

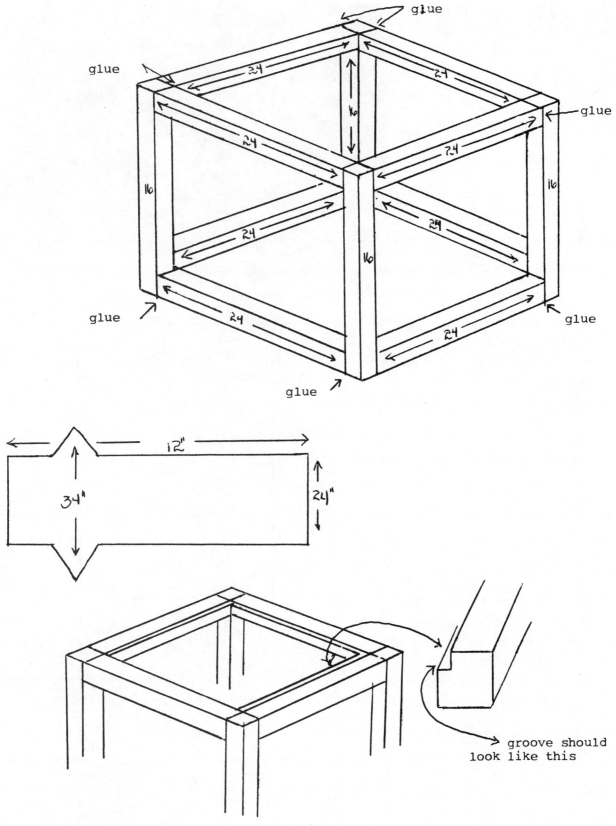

glue

glue

glue

glue

glue

glue

glue

24

24

24

24

24

24

24

24

16

16

16

16

16

12"

34"

24"

groove should
look like this

3 PLUMBER'S DREAM

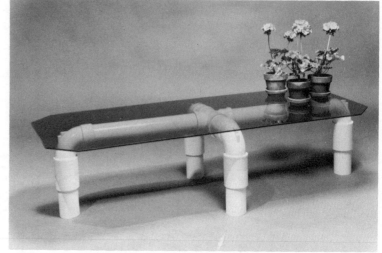

GREG PETERSEN

Materials

— **one** bronzed glass top, ¼" x 26" x 58¼"

— **four** rubber spacers

— **eight** PVC plastic piping, 3" diameter

— **four** elbows, PVC 3"

— **four** couplings, PVC 3"

— **two** T-joints

— epoxy

— white spray enamel

Tools

— fine-tooth wood saw

Method

Examine illustrations

— cut all piping according to length

— epoxy and fit all pieces together as shown

— spray paint

— fit glass top over base, using rubber spacers at corners to elevate glass approximately ¼"

Note: Legs may be left unglued from top frame and detached for easy storage. Many shapes and sizes may be obtained using this basic plan.

INSTRUCTIONS

MATERIALS- ¼" THICK (BRONZED) GLASS 58¼"x26"; 8' PVC PLASTIC PIPING (3"DIA.); 4 ELBOWS (PVC 3"); 4 COUPLINGS (3"PVC); 2 T-JOINTS; EPOXY; SPRAY ENAMEL (WHITE)

STEP 1. CUT ALL PIPING ACCORDING TO LENGTH.

2. EPOXY AND FIT ALL PIECES TOGETHER AS SHOWN.

3. SPRAY PAINT DESIRED COLOR (WHITE).

4. FIT GLASS TOP OVER FRAME USING RUBBER SPACERS AT CORNERS TO ELEVATE GLASS APPX. ¼".

NOTES.

MANY SHAPES AND SIZES MAY BE OBTAINED IN REGARDS TO FURNITURE USING THIS BASIC PLAN. MY TABLE'S OVERALL DIMENSIONS ARE APPX. 58"L x 26"W x 18¼" H. A FINE TOOTHED WOOD SAW MAY BE USED TO CUT THE PIPE. LEGS CAN BE LEFT UNGLUED FROM TOP FRAME AND DETACHED FOR EASY STORAGE. THE PIPE FITS VERY SNUG INTO THE JOINING MEMBERS. GLASS SHOULD BE THE LAST CONSIDERATION IN ORDER FOR A PROPER FIT. NO STILLSONS REQUIRED

5¾'

58¼"

GLASS TOP

26"

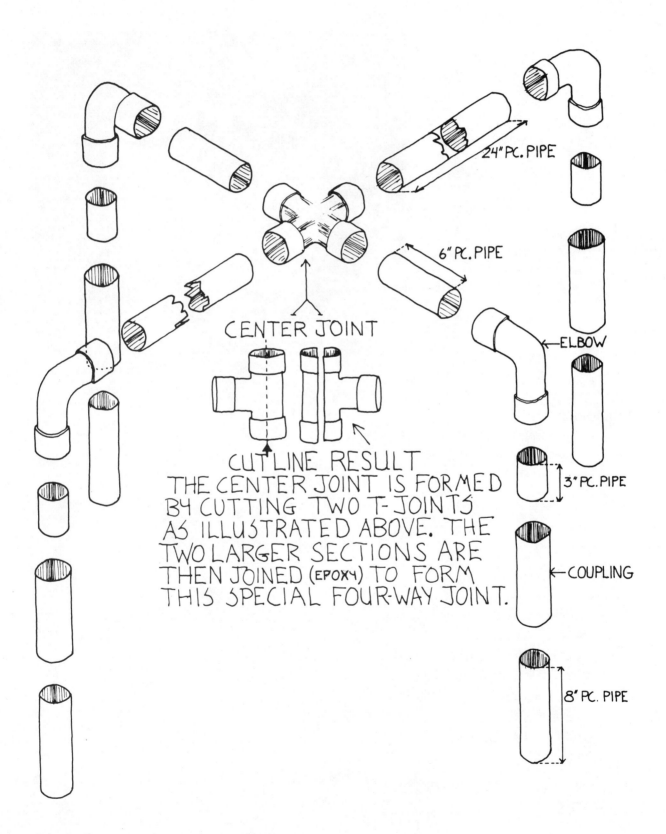

24" PC. PIPE

CENTER JOINT

6" PC. PIPE

ELBOW

CUT LINE RESULT
THE CENTER JOINT IS FORMED
BY CUTTING TWO T-JOINTS
AS ILLUSTRATED ABOVE. THE
TWO LARGER SECTIONS ARE
THEN JOINED (EPOXY) TO FORM
THIS SPECIAL FOUR-WAY JOINT.

3" PC. PIPE

COUPLING

8" PC. PIPE

4 COFFEE TABLE

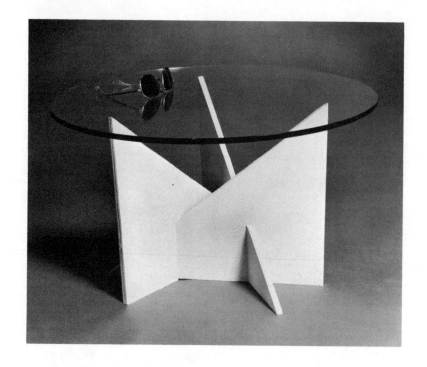

YUTAKA MATSUMOTO

Materials
— **one** piece plywood, ½" x 18" x 28"
— 24" diameter glass top ⅜" thick

Tools
— electric saw
— coping saw
— sandpaper

Method
Examine illustrations

— with electric saw, cut **three** triangles from plywood
— using electric saw and coping saw, make slits to fit each piece
— width of each slit is 1½" and slit is at 60° angle from surface
— join each piece little by little, then put on the glass top

Note: Try to make a paper model before starting.

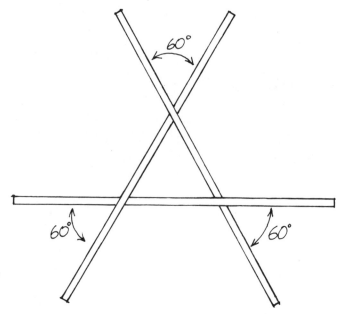

TOP VIEW

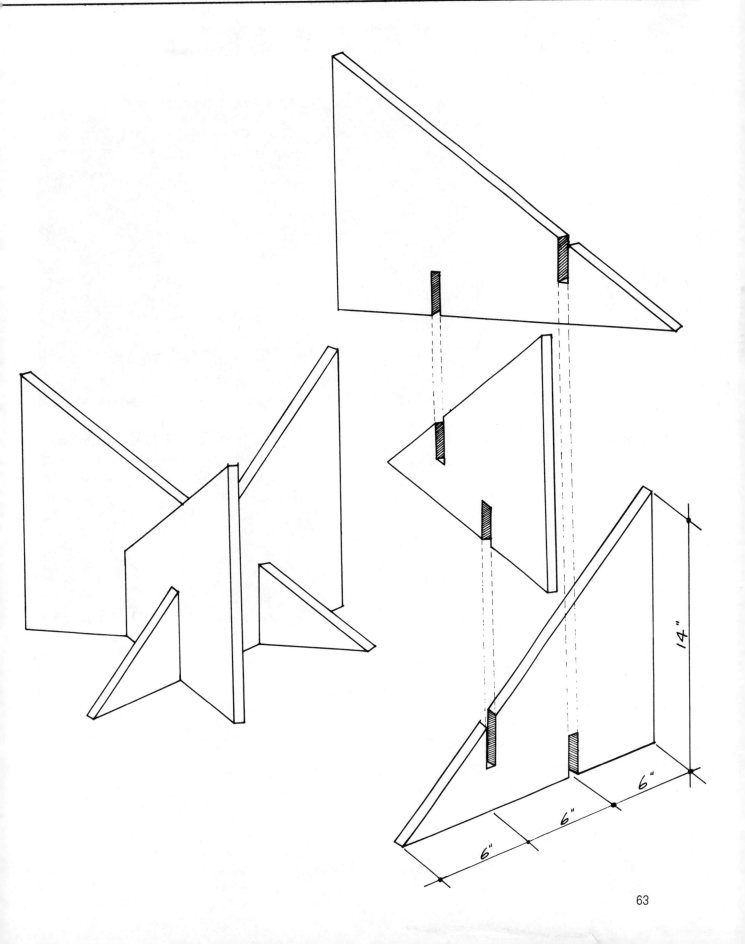

6"

6"

6"

14"

5 "O's" COFFEE TABLE

OLGA CRAIGEN

Materials
— **one** fiberglass planter, 14" diameter x 14" high*
— **one** circular bronze tinted glass top, ¾" thick x 42" diameter

Tools
— none needed

Method
Examine illustrations
— turn planter upside down
— with help of a friend, lift and center glass top on planter

  * available from Spiros Zakas, 252 Front Street, N.Y., N.Y. 10038

6 CUPID IN THE CLOUDS TABLE

REX WYNN

Materials

— **three** pieces pine, each ¾" x 11" x 16"
  (for table base)
— **two** pieces pine, each 1½" x 11" x 22"
  (to form circular table top) (from these
  two pieces, you will obtain four pieces
  of scrap)
— white glue
— finishing nails 1½" length
— **six** finishing nails 2" length
— 13 oz. can flat white spray paint
— 13 oz. can light blue spray paint
— tube white acrylic
— tube yellow acrylic
— tube blue acrylic
— tube yellow ochre

Tools

— pencil
— ruler
— jigsaw
— sandpaper, fine & coarse
— brushes, #3 and #8
— masking tape

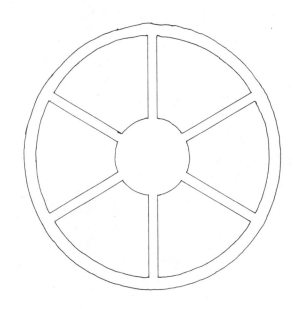

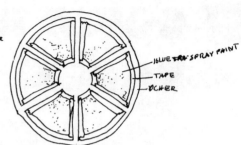

PAINTING INSTRUCTIONS FOR TOP

BLUE — SPRAY PAINT
TAPE
OCHER

CUPID SHOULD BE ABOUT ½ WAY UP THE BASE
HAIR AN WINGS ABOUT ¼ WAY DOWN FROM TOP

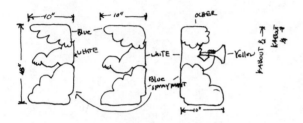

BLUE
WHITE
WHITE
OCHER
Yellow
BLUE — SPRAY PAINT
ABOUT 2 ½"

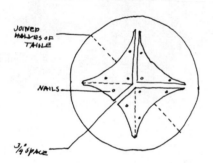

JOINED HALVES OF TABLE
NAILS
¾" SPACE

CONSTRUCTION INSTRUCTIONS FOR BOTTOM

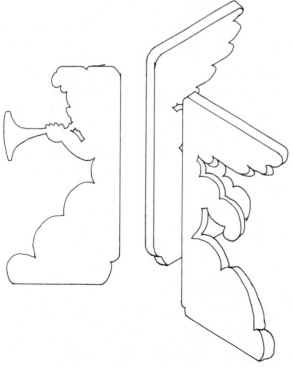

Method

Examine illustrations

— draw pattern on **three** pieces of ¾" x 11" x 16" pine

— draw **two** 22" diameter semicircles on **two** pieces of 1½" x 11" x 22" pine

— with jigsaw, cut out pieces of scrap from circular top material

— take **one** of **four** pieces of scrap and cut this in half (you now have **five** pieces of scrap)

— sand all pieces smooth

— with glue, join two semicircles to form circular top

— glue and nail (2" nails) scraps to circular top

— spray white paint on entire table top (top and bottom) and **three** pieces of table base; let dry

— spray table top with light blue paint to get a cloud effect; let dry

— cover white and light blue areas with masking tape; then paint yellow ochre design; let dry

— remove tape

— paint base following same procedure as above

— fit **three** base pieces into slots (formed with **five** pieces of scrap) at bottom of table top

— the figure of the head should be placed in the slot between the piece of scrap cut in half

— glue

— let dry

7 MOP ART TABLE

SPIROS ZAKAS

Materials
— wire lamp shade frame
— "Mop Art" mops*
— glass top

Tools
— none needed

Method
Examine illustrations
— begin with a wire lamp shade frame that
   is in proportion with your seating
— cover the frame with mops all around
— take the first layer of mop strands (from
   the outside rim of the frame) and overlay
   them across the opening at the top
— as each mop strand is overlaid, a
   valance effect at the top of the wire lamp
   shade frame is created
— place glass top on top of covered wire
   lamp shade frame which now acts as
   the base of table

Note: These "Mop Art" mops may be
dyed using cold water dyes, available in
bright beautiful colors. Thread mop strands
with wood beads or tortoise-shell bangles
if you like.

* Available only from Spiros Zakas, 252
Front Street, N.Y., N.Y. 10038

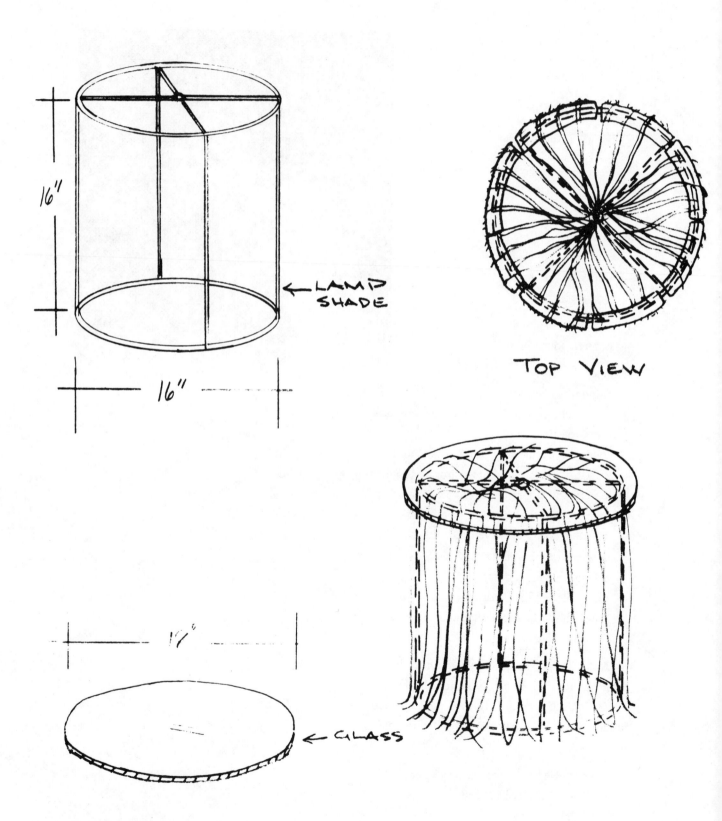

16"

16"

← LAMP
SHADE

TOP VIEW

12"

← GLASS

SMALL STUFF

We shouldn't forget that the little ones on our planet live on a different scale. They have their needs too. Everyone has the usual little rocker, stool, or bed—but it's also nice to have a little fantasy.

Children live on clouds, in sand castles, on trees, in doll houses, and on trains. Their world is big and small and it's nice to re-create it for them.

Depending on how you cut it, plywood can be the means of constructing endless imaginative projects. We hope you find some of our ideas useful in fashioning the fantasies of your own small stuff.

TOAD STOOL

REX WYNN

Materials

— **one** piece plywood, ¾'' x 2' x 4'
— fabric, 4' square
— foam rubber, 5'' thick x 2 in. diameter
— tube of permanent light green acrylic paint
— **eight** nails, 1¼''

Tools

— pencil
— ruler
— jigsaw
— paint brushes, #3 and #8
— staple gun

Method

Examine illustrations
— draw **three** pieces on plywood
— cut out
— paint base
— join **two** pieces into slots
— nail circular top to base
— lay foam on seat top
— center fabric over foam so that corners of fabric will extend down, approximately 1' at each corner, to spaces in between base
— staple **four** corners of fabric to base (there are **eight** places)
— with remaining loose fabric, pleat as you staple

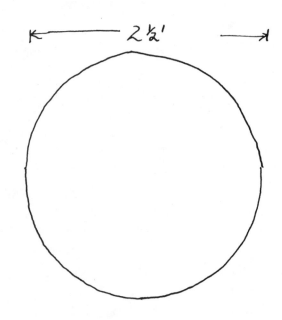

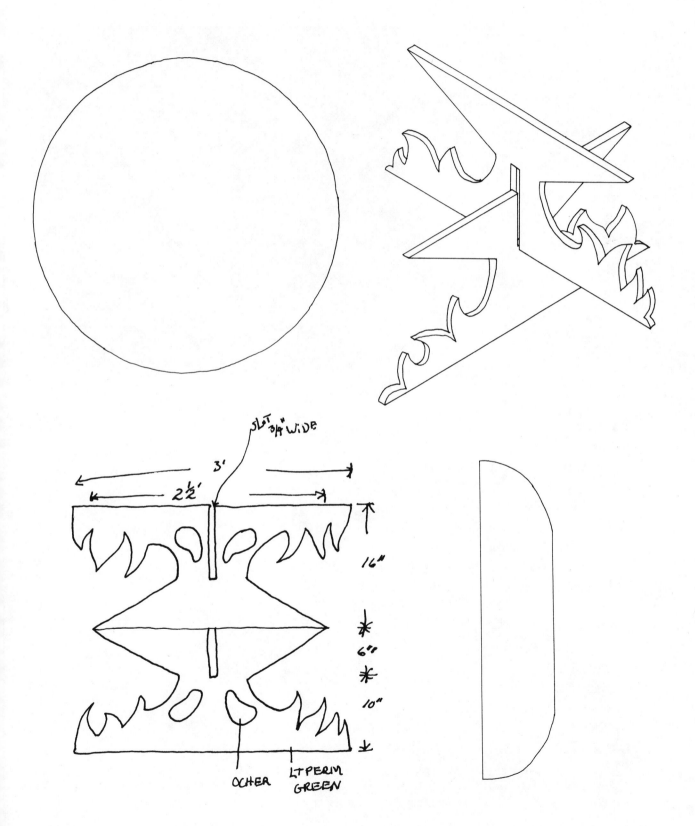

SLOT 3/4" WIDE

3'

2½'

16"

✳

6"

✳

10"

✳

OCHER   LT PERM GREEN

2 GAME CUBE

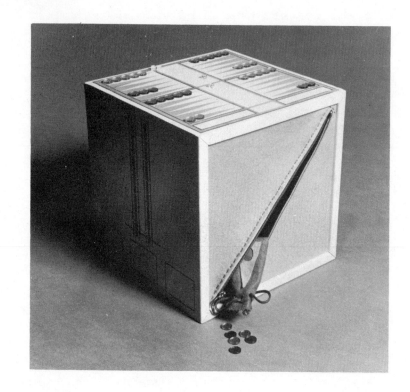

STEPHANIE DIETERICH

Materials

— **one** piece clear pine, 1″ x 12″ x 5′
— flat screen mold, ¾″ thick x 8′ long
— casein glue
— mustard yellow felt, ⅓ yard x 60″ wide
— **two** ring zippers, each 14″ long
— red embroidery thread
— rubber cement
— finishing nails, 4 penny
— wire brads, ¾″ x 20″
— plastic wood
— ½ pt. primer
— **four** cans yellow paint (Testers spray paint #1214)
— **two** cans red paint (Testers spray paint #1204)
— Testers brush-on paint to match colors above, for touchups

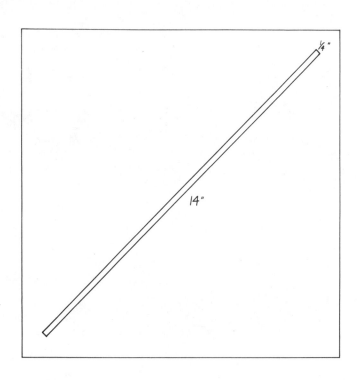

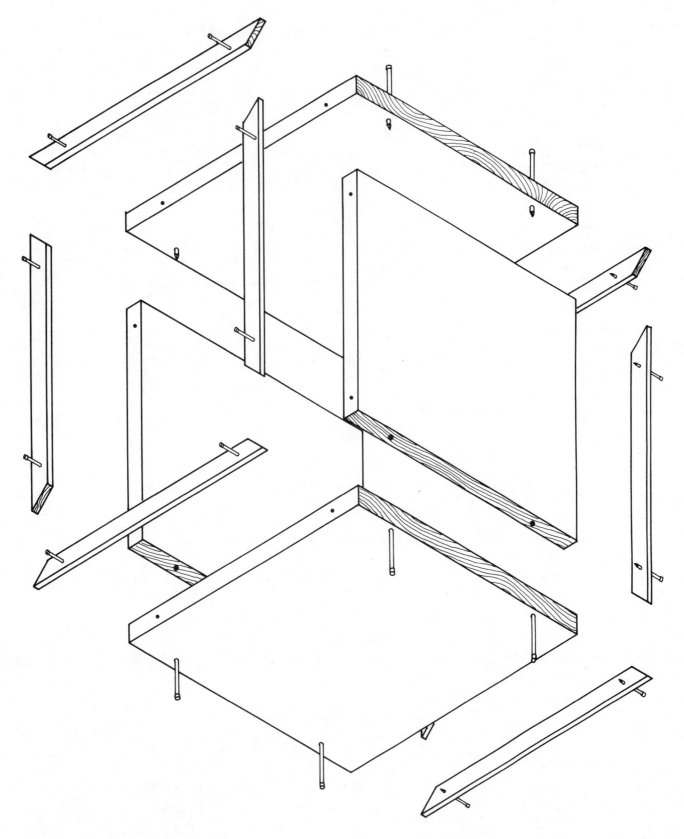

Tools

— sandpaper
— damp sponge
— table saw
— C-clamps
— wood blocks
— belt sander
— small miter box
— nail set
— hammer
— Exacto knife, #11 blade
— masking tape
— ochre magic marker
— pencil and ruler
— crewel needle
— scissors

Method

Examine illustrations

— sand both sides of the board
— cut clear pine into **four** pieces, each 12" x 12"
— glue and nail together with finishing nails; set nails
— apply C clamps and wood blocks and wipe off excess glue with damp sponge
— sand outside of box with belt sander
— miter the flat screen mold to fit edges of cube
— tack flat screen mold to cube with wire brads (marking each piece of flat screen mold and its place on cube so that you can remove them later on, and then replace them permanently)
— sand the flat screen mold so that it is flush with the game cube
— apply primer inside and out

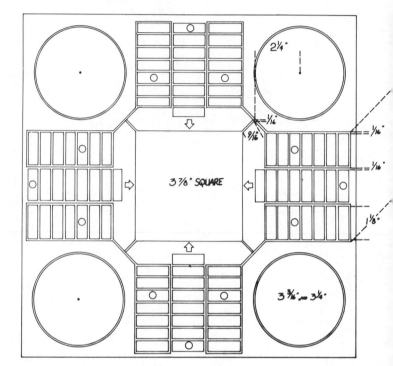

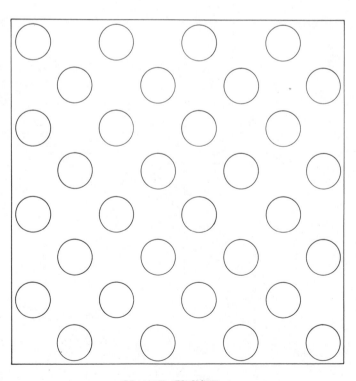

ORANGE FRISKET

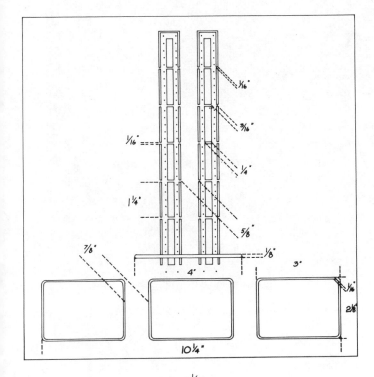

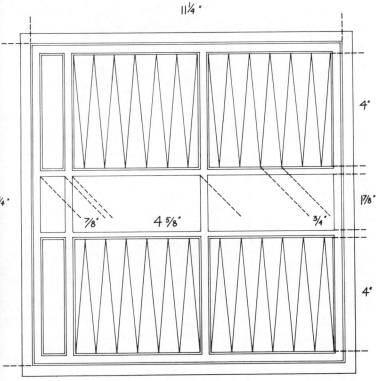

— fill any holes with plastic wood; let dry, and sand
— sand, by hand, the entire cube
— apply **two** or **three** coats of yellow spray paint, sanding as necessary.
— stain cloth part of zippers with ochre marker; let dry
— mask the entire cloth part of zippers with tape; spray exposed parts with red spray paint; let dry, then remove masking tape
— cut with Exacto knife **two** 11¾" squares out of mustard felt; cut diagonal strip in each, to match perimeter of zipper
— sew zippers in with embroidery thread and crewel needle using running stitches
— remove flat screen mold from cube and rubber cement felt squares onto open sides of cube
— replace flat screen mold, hammer down and set brads
— fill in holes with plastic wood, sand, and touch up with yellow paint

Note: You may apply store-bought game boards to the four sides of your cube. (The designer made all four game boards—chess, backgammon, parchesi, and cribbage.) You may purchase game pieces, which can be conveniently stored inside cube. A few illustrations of her work on the game boards are shown.

3 ROCKING GOAT

STEPHANIE DIETERICH

Materials

— **two** pieces brown wrapping paper,
   24'' x 24''
— masking tape
— **one** strip narrow light cardboard, 10''
   long
— **one** piece plywood, ¾'' x 4' x 4'
— **six** sheets carbon paper
— **one** piece clear pine, 5/4'' x 3'' x 4'
— white glue
— closet pole, 1½'' diameter x 2' long
— **one** empty paper towel roll
— finishing nails, 1½''
— plastic wood
— sandpaper, fine
— **one** pt. latex primer
— **one** pt. white latex enamel
— red felt ½ yard
— 100' reinforced cotton clothesline

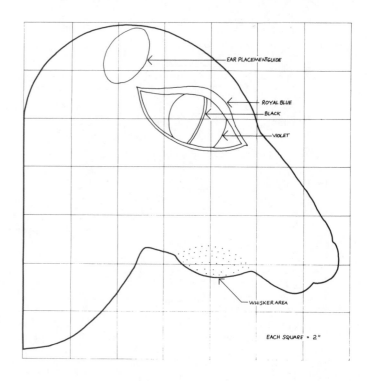

EAR PLACEMENT GUIDE

ROYAL BLUE
BLACK

VIOLET

WHISKER AREA

EACH SQUARE = 2"

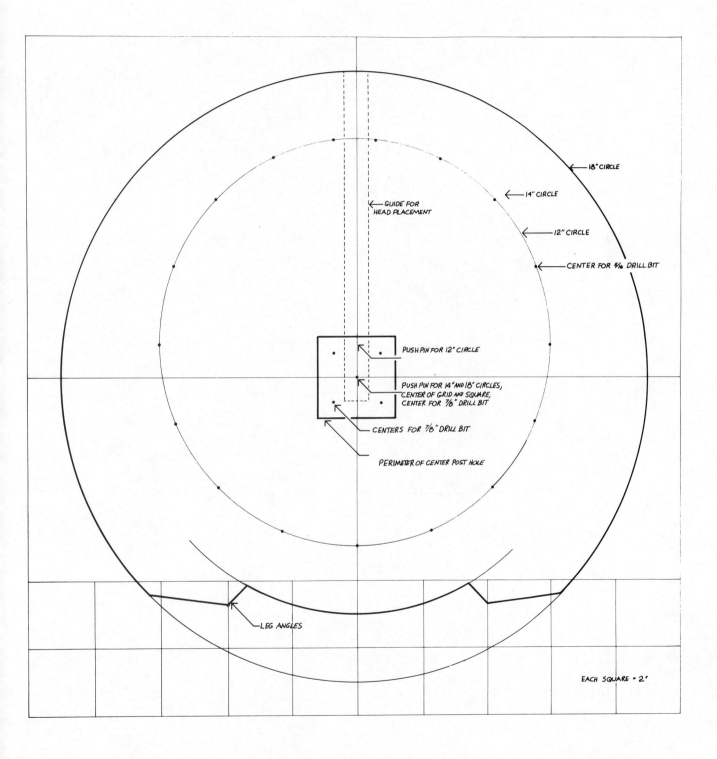

18" CIRCLE

14" CIRCLE

12" CIRCLE

CENTER FOR 5/16 DRILL BIT

GUIDE FOR
HEAD PLACEMENT

PUSH PIN FOR 12" CIRCLE

PUSH PIN FOR 14" AND 18" CIRCLES,
CENTER OF GRID AND SQUARE,
CENTER FOR 7/8" DRILL BIT

CENTERS FOR 7/8" DRILL BIT

PERIMETER OF CENTER POST HOLE

LEG ANGLES

EACH SQUARE = 2"

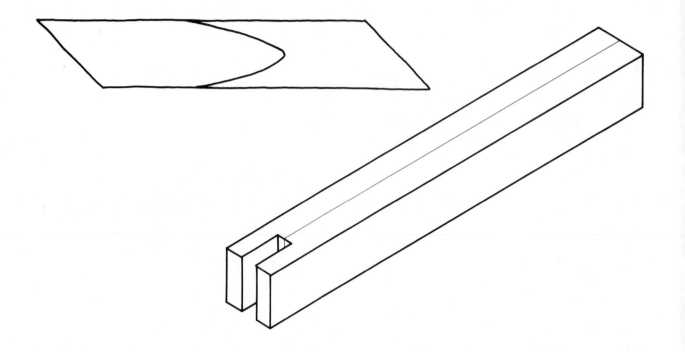

Tools

— pencil
— ruler
— yardstick
— beam compass
— table saw
— **four** blocks wood
— two C clamps
— power planer
— belt sander
— band saw
— drill press
— **two** pinch clamps
— saber saw
— Exacto knife, #11 blade
— damp sponge
— hammer
— nail set
— paint brush
— felt tip markers (black, royal blue, and violet)

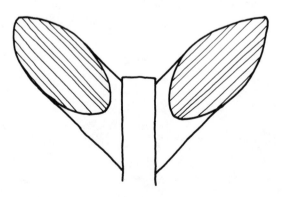

Method

Examine illustrations

— tape piece of brown paper (24" x 24") to table with masking tape

— draw 2" grid

— transfer outline of head, ear placement guide, eye, and whisker area to paper grid

— tape piece of brown paper (24" x 24") to table with masking tape

— with yardstick, draw 20" square with lines running through center in vertical and horizontal directions

— at bottom of square, draw double row 2" grid

— with beam compass scribe an 18"-diameter circle in center-point of 20" square

— with beam compass, scribe an arc at bottom of square 7" down from center point

— place compass exactly 1" above center spot; scribe a 12"-diameter circle

— transfer drill bit centers along circumference of 12"-diameter circle

— transfer dotted line (in head placement)

— transfer 2⅜" square center post hole or opening

— transfer ⅞" drill bit guides in square

— transfer leg angles

— on table saw, cut ¾" plywood into **four** pieces, 2' x 2' each

— with carbon paper, transfer everything from pattern to plywood

— remove papers from wood and drill bit centers along circle as marked: square at center, bit centers in square

— cut **two** 22" pieces from clear pine for center post

— glue and clamp together (use wood blocks to protect furniture surface); let dry

— with power planer, plane down center post until it is square (approx. 2⅜" sq.)

— sand with belt sander

— on table saw, cut slot (¾" x 2") in center front end

— with band saw, cut outline of head

— with drill press and 3/16" bit (to accommodate whisker strings), drill as many holes in whisker area as is practical

— with pinch clamps, clamp **two** rocker squares together with marked square on top

— with band saw, cut outline; keep pieces clamped together

— with drill press and 5/16" bit, drill holes as marked along 12" diameter circle

— check dimensions of your center post with dimensions of square drawn on rocker (adjust the drawn square if necessary)

— with drill press and ⅞" bit, drill holes as marked in square

— with saber saw, starting in drilled holes, cut out square along drawn or adjusted perimeter

— using Exacto knife and paper towel roll experiment with the angles for the making of the ears

— when you have all angles cut, transfer angle information to the closet pole

— on table saw, cut the short angles at either end of closet pole

— cut long angle

— force back rocker (one with no markings) onto the unslotted end of the center

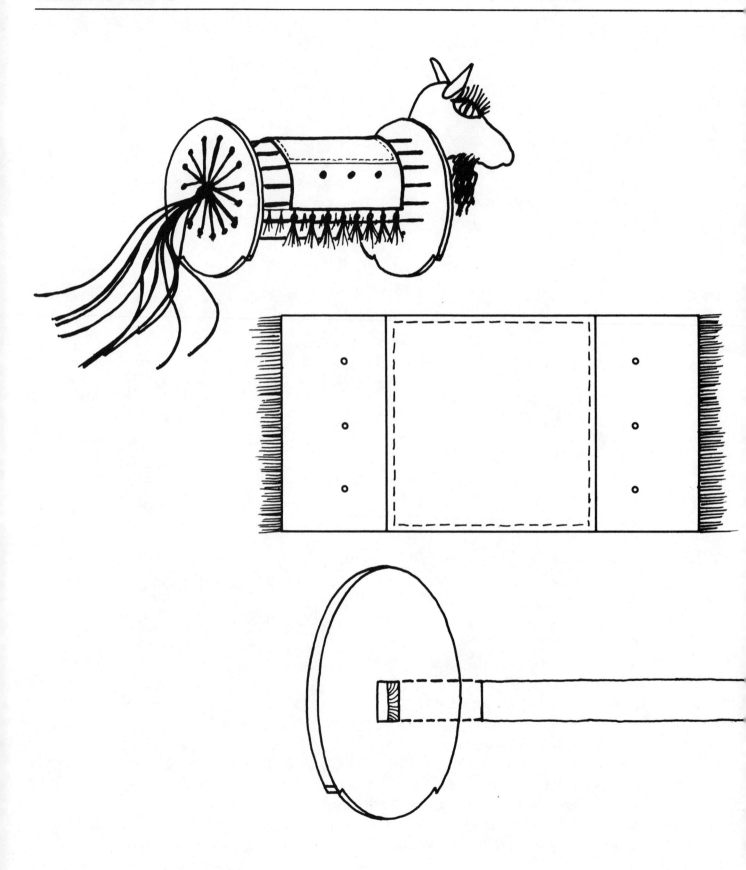

post so that the post protrudes 1″ from the other side (use glue for tight fit; wipe away excess glue with damp sponge)

— force other rocker onto other end of post (marked side to the front), so that 2″ of post protrudes

— spike ears to head with 1½″ finishing nails; set nails

— apply white glue to slot in center post and within head placement guidelines

— place head in position; spike with finishing nails; set nails; wipe away excess glue

— fill any holes or gouges with plastic wood; let dry, and sand

— sand away any visible carbon paper marks, rough spots and edges of plywood

— prime; let dry

— apply white latex enamel; let dry

— with carbon paper and paper head pattern, trace eye lightly onto both sides of head

— using felt tip marker, color eyes as indicated

— cut felt triangles, 2″ long and ½″ at base

— roll each triangle from pointed end to large end, and squish; unroll (they should be curly)

— glue broad ends of triangles (lashes) along upper edge of royal blue outline

— cut sisal cord into 1′ lengths (as many as you drilled holes for)

— thread sisal through holes, knotting close to head on both sides

— trim and shape board

— cut clothesline into 4½′ lengths (**seventeen** of them)

— knot one end of clothesline and string it through rockers from front through back

— pull tight and knot at back

— when all holes are strung, gather all tail ends except for one strand at bottom

— pull tight, centering bunch at protruding center post

— wrap and secure bunch with the loose bottom strand

Optional: see illustration

— make a saddle to fit rocker

4 FOREST ROOM DIVIDER

REX WYNN

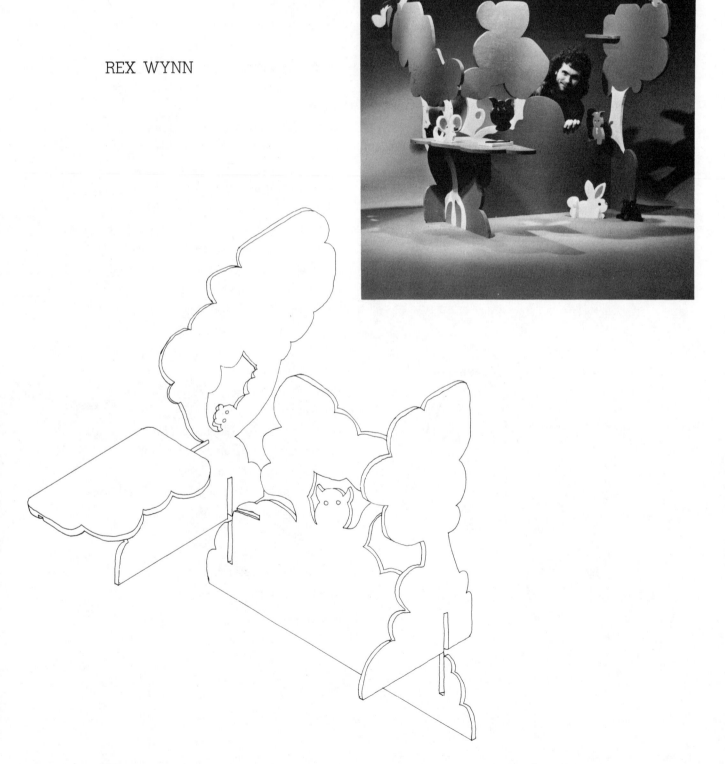

Materials

— plywood, ¾'' x 4' x 8', to form **four** pieces
— jar permanent light-green acrylic paint
— jar zinc white
— tube red acrylic
— tube yellow acrylic
— tube blue acrylic
— tube brown acrylic
— tube green acrylic
— tube orange acrylic

Tools

— jigsaw
— pencil
— circular saw
— drill

— three brushes, 2'', #3, and #8
— sandpaper

Method

Examine illustrations

— draw pattern on plywood
— measure in ¾'' wide slots
— with jigsaw, cut out slots
— use drill to begin eyes
— using circular saw, make dotto in table top and in owl section
— sand plywood structure
— paint design
— assemble **four** pieces of plywood
— make additional animals with scraps

5 CLOUD CHAIR

CAROLYN CRAWFORD

Materials
— **two** pieces plywood, ¾" x 4' x 6'
— **ten** supports, ¾" x 2" x 11"
— **six** risers, ¾" x 2" x 24"
— **five** step seats, ¾" x 12" x 24"
— **forty** screws, 1", flathead, countersunk screws
— small bottle white glue
— **one** qt. blue latex paint
— 328 silver studs

Optional
— **three** yards fabric, 36" wide
— **four** rolls foam, 2" x 24" x 6'
— 196 upholstery tacks

Tools
— hammer
— jigsaw
— sandpaper
— paint brush
— screwdriver

Optional
— staple gun
— scissors

Method
Examine illustrations
— using dimensions shown, draw cloud shapes on plywood (use large kitchen plates or bowls as templates)
— use jigsaw to cut out curved cloud shapes (**two** pieces of plywood to have identical cloud shapes)
— sand edges of saw cuts and flat surfaces

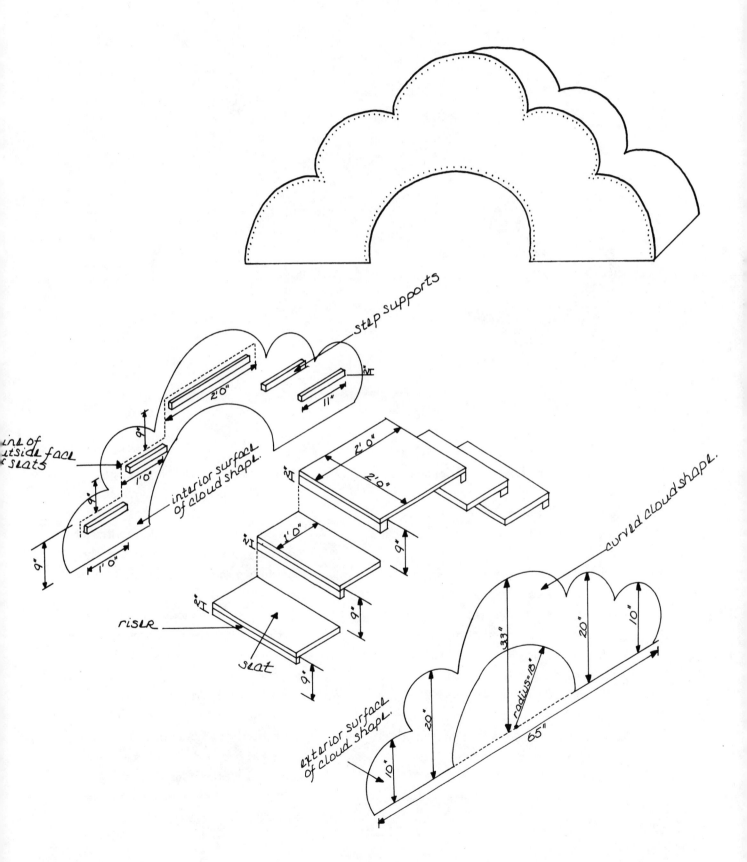

step supports

line of
outside face
of slats

interior surface
of cloud shape

2' 0"

9"

1' 0"

9"

1' 0"

11"

1½"

2' 0"

2' 0"

1½"

9"

1½"

1' 0"

9"

riser

slat

1½"

9"

curved cloud shape

exterior surface
of cloud shape

10"

20"

33"

radius=10"

20"

10"

65"

10"

— screw supports to insides of both cloud
  shapes
— assisted by a friend, align cloud shapes
  in upright position, and screw steps onto
  supports
— glue each riser along its top edge to the
  underside of each step
— glue riser ends to inside of cloud shapes
— remove dust and debris; paint cloud
  chair with blue latex paint; let dry
— tack silver studs along cloud curves,
  1″ away from curve edges and
  approximately 1″ apart

Optional (if you're still feeling ambitious,
  you can upholster interior of Cloud
  Chair)

— wrap foam around each step, stapling
  foam ends on underside of step

— using cloud shape as template, lay
  cloud shape on its side and outline
  curves on sheet of foam
— cut foam and staple to inside surface of
  two cloud shapes (it is easier to apply
  foam in **two** sections, above and below
  step)
— wrap fabric around foam and around
  stapling fabric ends on underside of step
  (fabric cover will be applied only to
  inside surfaces of the two cloud shapes)
— take fabric and fold under ¾″ and tack
  along outside edge of cloud shape
— bring fabric over and down the inside
  surface of each side until it meets the
  steps; tuck fabric under fabric of steps
  (friction of two fabric pieces is sufficient
  to hold them in place)

6 LITTLE PEOPLE'S LOVE SEAT

CAROLYN CRAWFORD

Materials
— **two** pieces plywood, each ¾" x 4' x 6'
— **two** piano hinges
— **twelve** small L-shaped metal brackets
— glue
— wood screws, ½"
— jars of acrylic paint (white, red, brown, yellow)

Tools
— pencil
— ruler
— jigsaw
— screwdriver
— paint brush

Method
Examine illustrations

— using dimensions shown, draw figures on plywood; when finished, this will form back of love seat (the seat itself is a rectangular box consisting of a back, a front, two sides, a bottom, and a hinged top; the hinged top is the seat as well as access storage)
— cut the above pieces according to the dimensions shown
— glue front, bottom, and side box.pieces together
— when all is dry, attach back to box
— screw metal brackets inside of box for reinforcement
— paint figures on face of plywood as shown
— hinge seat to back piece

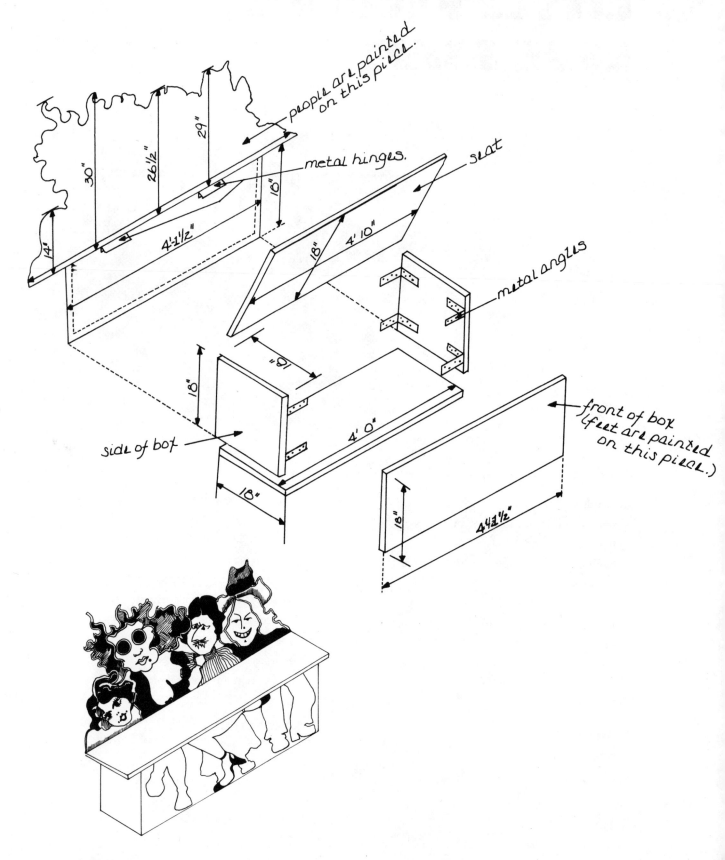

people are painted on this piece.

metal hinges.

slat

30"

26½"

29"

10"

14"

4'-1½"

18"

4' 10"

metal angles

18"

16"

side of box

4' 0"

18"

front of box
(feet are painted
on this piece.)

18"

4'4½"

7 TENSEGRITY STOOL

DAVID FLEISCHER

Materials
— **three** ¾″ wood dowels, 32″ long
— ½ yd. heavy canvas
— 14 ft. 4″ nylon parachute cord
— **three** rubber cane tips

Tools
— drill with ¼″ drill bit
— sewing machine (or just a needle and thread)
— saw
— grommetter

Method
— cut **three** ⅝″ dowels at 32″ length
— using a ¼″ bit, drill **two** holes in **each dowel**
— wrap a rubber band around the center of the **three** sticks; this should help you hold them upright as you tie them together
— lace the sticks together in alternate pairs using a "three sides complete" rectangular pattern
— now complete the pattern by closing off the top of the octagon that the string is forming

   Note: This octagon of nylon string is the tension element of the structure; the wood dowels compress the structure. The balance between tension and compression is the reason the whole thing works.

— draw a 19″ equilateral triangle (a triangle in which each angle equals 60 degrees) on your canvas
— cut out the 19″ triangle and sew up about a half inch hem (so the thread won't unravel)
— now fold the corners up to the 17″ mark and grommet them so that they are now sturdy triangular pockets for the dowels to go into
— sew up the rest of the hem along the 17″ line
— put the rubber cups on the bottom of the stool legs; put the seat on top

8 THE TEDDY BEAR CHAIR

MARY L. COWAN

Materials

— **one** piece ¾″ plywood, 42″ x 48″
— white glue, medium-size bottle
— **thirty** 1½″ finishing nails
— **one** 1″ diameter wooden dowel, 36″ long
— **three** double-sided metal pipe holders, 1″ (see illustration)
— **six** ¾″ screws
— **one** qt. polyfoam cement
— **one** piece 3″ foam, 3′ x 6′
— **one** piece 2″ foam, 36″ x 37″
— **two** bolsters, foam, 20″ long x 32″ in circumference (for legs)
— **two** bolsters, foam, 24″ long x 28″ in circumference (for arms)
— **ten** lbs. fiber-fill
— **six** yds. fake fur, 60″ wide
— **one** spool heavy-duty thread (large size) for machine stitching
— **one** spool carpet thread for hand stitching
— **one** oz. wool yarn, **four** fold, black
— **two** 1½″ buttons, black
— **one** roll craft paper or butcher paper, 48″ long

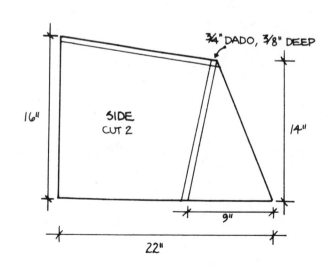

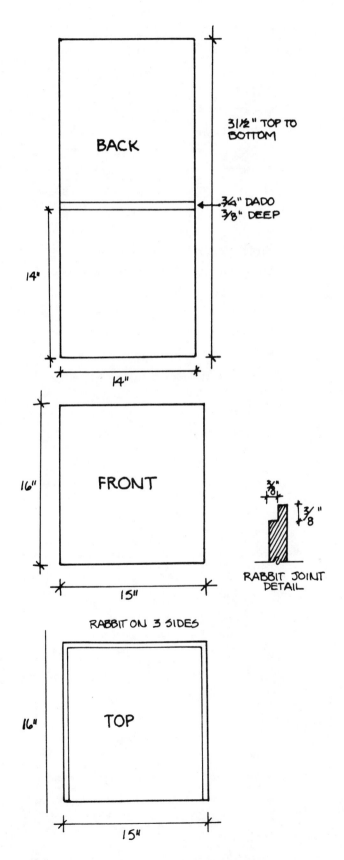

BACK

31½" TOP TO BOTTOM

¾" DADO
⅜" DEEP

14"

14"

FRONT

16"

15"

RABBIT ON 3 SIDES

⅜"

⅜"

RABBIT JOINT
DETAIL

TOP

16"

15"

— **one** package yellow blanket seam binding (4¾ yds.)

Tools

— circular table saw
— saw blades, 8" or 10", to combine to make ⅜" and ¾" cuts
— **four** adjustable cabinetmaker clamps, 24" long
— hammer
— screwdriver
— tape measure or yardstick
— straight edge
— bread knife or serrated blade at least 12" long
— **one** crummy brush (wrap when not in use for cement, and freeze; it will become pliable again when defrosted)
— sewing machine
— scissors
— 4" card
— carpet needle
— pencil or marker
— pins
— iron

Method

wood frame

— cut wood pieces as per dimensions with circular saw
— set blades at ¾" for dado joints, ⅜" from table top; draw dado on inside pieces ¾" wide with straight edge
— begin the dado 9" from back angled corner, drawing a line to the top corner; cut
— measure and draw dado of some above dimensions on back piece, 14" from bottom of back piece
— set blades for ⅜" rabbit joint, ⅜" from table top

— rabbit top edges of sides, and **three** sides of top seat piece

— apply white glue generously to back dado; fit in the top seat where it is not dadoed

— glue generously dados of side pieces and rabbits; fit back and seat top to the sides

— turn on side and clamp down to table on **four** corners

— nail about every 3" with finishing nails where all rabbit joints meet

— unclamp and glue front piece generously, and apply to top seat and sides

— nail as above on **three** sides

— turn back on side, clamp down and set overnight

— place dowel in the middle of the back piece, on the back side, so that 15" rise above the back of the seat

— evenly space the pipe holders 4" apart; mark where the holes for the screws appear (pinch them in a bit to secure the dowel)

— begin the hole slightly with a nail, then screw in each pipe holder tightly

— hammer in finishing nails at bottom (1), and between the pipe holders

— cut **four** arm patterns; leave opening where indicated on pattern for turning and stuffing; stitch and turn

— fill out roundness of shoulder and paw with fiber-fill

— stuff in 24" bolster; fill out with fiber-fill where not firm

— blind-stitch the opening by hand; set aside

— cut **four** leg patterns; stitch, leaving opening where indicated on the pattern; turn out

— fill out roundness with fiber-fill at hip and front leg

— stuff 20" bolster into form; fill out where not firm; blind-stitch by hand at opening; set aside

— cut **two** head side pieces

— cut face and head front (pattern can be pieced where indicated on the pattern); allowance is made at the back of the neck for any extra seaming

— beginning at bottom neck, pin face and head front to head sides

— stitch with sewing machine using heavy-duty thread at seam lines indicated on pattern; turn out

— stuff **firmly** at snout (the headrest) using fiber fill; then keep stuffing until the head takes firm shape

— fit onto dowel, checking for placement of headrest

— fold under excess fabric all around head; secure front of neck first with carpet thread, then continue to blind-stitch all around neck

— cut **four** ears; stitch at seam lines indicated on pattern; stitch and turn

— place onto head and pin, turning under row edges; spread out ears about 2" to create fullness

foam padding

Note: All "edges" refer to the thickness of the foam, either 2" or 3". Polyfoam cement must be applied to **all** surfaces to be joined. Allow at least thirty seconds to let cement set up.

— cut 3" foam 48" long with bread knife to cover seat and sides

— paint polyfoam cement on seat frame, sides, and on one side of foam using a crummy brush; allow cement to set

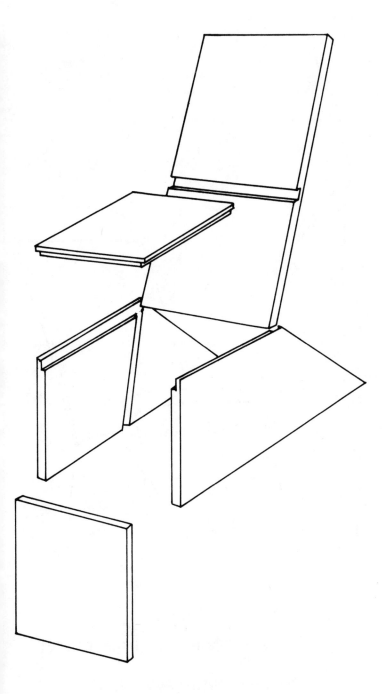

— wrap foam around seat, aligning foam
edge to seat back from side to side
(there will be an overlap of foam at seat
front)
— at corners of chair frame, draw a wedge
to be 2" at widest point at foam edge,
to the point of the chair frame
— cut with knife to seat corners and
remove the wedges, to be made at front
two corners only
— cement front chair frame and inside
foam, which will fold over to the front of
the chair frame; press down (don't
worry if the foam does not fit exactly as
the body of the bear is created from
the stuffing process)
— cement top overlap underside and the
area it will cover; fold over and press
down
— take remainder of foam, 26" x 36", and
wrap around the back of the chair to
meet both edges of side foam
— cement edges of side foam and back
foam; attach one side, then pull around
to the other side
— take 2" foam, 30" wide x 36" long;
measure from the bottom at the center
up 15½" and make a hole or slit for the
dowel
— slip foam over dowel, cement edge to
seat at front, and edge to back at back
foam edge
— align 2" foam to 3" foam on outside
profile
— pinch corners in with finger to form
roundness; cement where foam meets at
the pinch, and on edges of the front
and back foam
— press together in alignment front and
back edges of both right and left sides

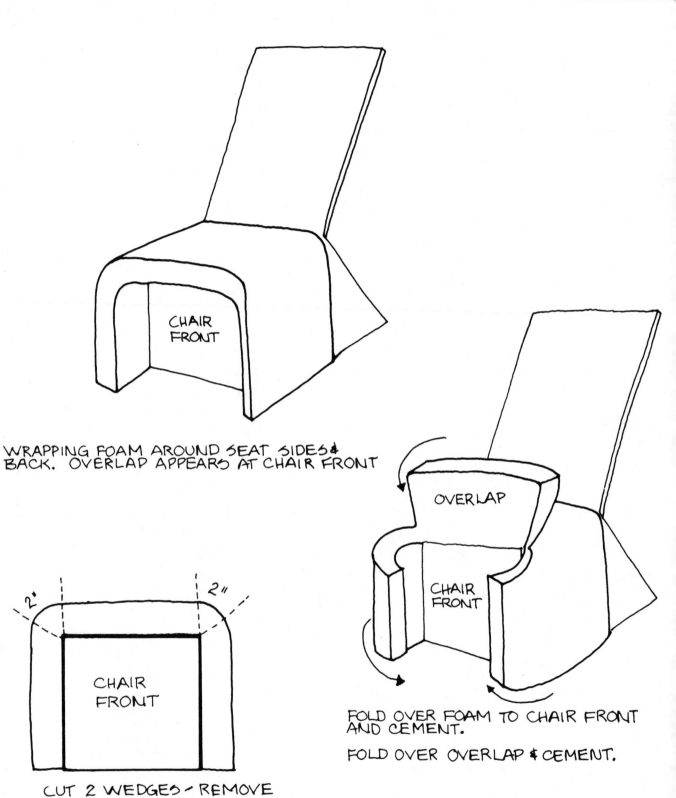

CHAIR
FRONT

WRAPPING FOAM AROUND SEAT SIDES &
BACK. OVERLAP APPEARS AT CHAIR FRONT

OVERLAP

CHAIR
FRONT

FOLD OVER FOAM TO CHAIR FRONT
AND CEMENT.

FOLD OVER OVERLAP & CEMENT.

2"   2"

CHAIR
FRONT

CUT 2 WEDGES - REMOVE

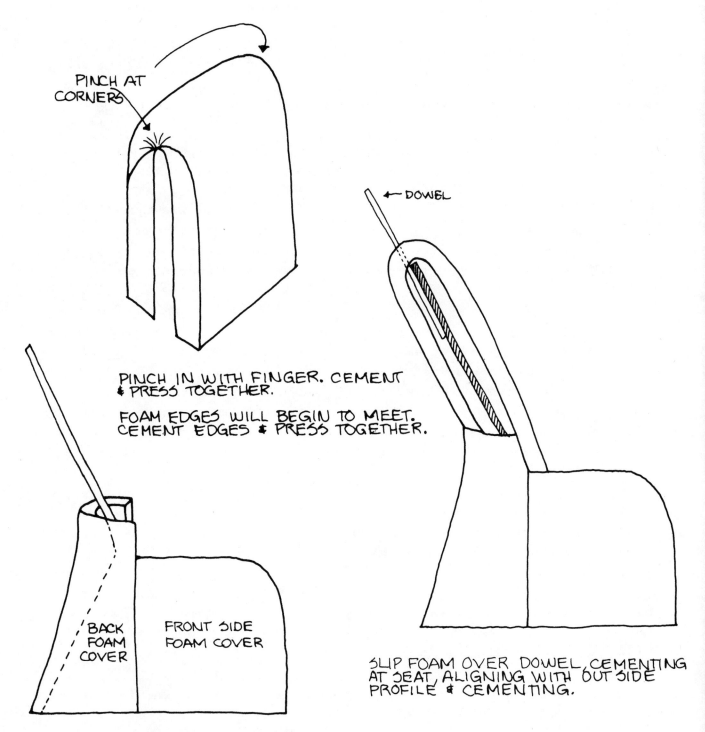

PINCH AT CORNERS

DOWEL

PINCH IN WITH FINGER. CEMENT & PRESS TOGETHER.

FOAM EDGES WILL BEGIN TO MEET. CEMENT EDGES & PRESS TOGETHER.

BACK FOAM COVER

FRONT SIDE FOAM COVER

SLIP FOAM OVER DOWEL, CEMENTING AT SEAT, ALIGNING WITH OUTSIDE PROFILE & CEMENTING.

ALIGN 2" BACK FOAM WITH FRONT 3" FOAM.

WRAP AROUND BACK OF CHAIR

of the foam

— make a lumbar support from the remaining 2" foam which will be 7" wide x 30" long, using the bread knife to cut

— place at 4½" from depressed seat, or where the small of your back is located

— cement both foam surfaces and press down

fabric cover

Note: All seam allowances are ⅝". Pattern pieces are sewn by machine. If the fabric has a nap, make sure it is running in the same direction. Place pattern pieces as close together as possible.

— with craft paper, make a grid of 1" squares to form 8" blocks and copy pattern from book to enlarged grid

— cut out pattern pieces

— fold material with right sides together

— place **back** at center line on the fold to cut **one** piece

— place and pin **front belly** at center line on fold line to cut **one** piece

— place and pin **two side** pieces; cut out

— with right sides together, pin **back** to **sides** and stitch on seam lines indicated on the pattern

— with right sides together, pin **front belly** to **sides,** leaving an opening on one side about 12" long where indicated on the pattern

— stitch and turn out body form to the right side

— pull over chair from the top (at the shoulder, the material should not totally encase the foam understructure)

— stuff rump with fiber-fill from bottom of seat, filling out cloth form **firmly**

— stuff front of chair from bottom to fill out form

— stuff chest and shoulders from top opening

— stuff sides and seat from 12" opening, evening out the fiber-fill to prevent lumps

— when body looks firm and filled out fully, blind-stitch opening with carpet thread by hand

— blind-stitch all around ears

— to make nose, take the yarn and wrap it around the 4" card until all the yarn is used up; pull off card and tie securely at the middle, holding onto the ties

— clip loops on both sides and fluff out to form a hemisphere

— with scissors, clip the yarn until it forms a perfect half sphere

— at the knot, stitch onto snout with carpet thread

— glue underside of nose with white glue and press down the bottom yarn

— sew on buttons for eyes

— to attach legs, blind-stitch all around securely with carpet thread by hand

— to attach arms, begin at shoulder, adjust for armrest height, and blind-stitch all around where arm meets body

— to make bow, measure around neck of bear (should be about 57")

— mark the 57" dimension in the center of the seam binding; press out the fold at both ends, which will create a fuller bow

— tie the double fold binding around neck; tie the bow out of the ironed-out ends

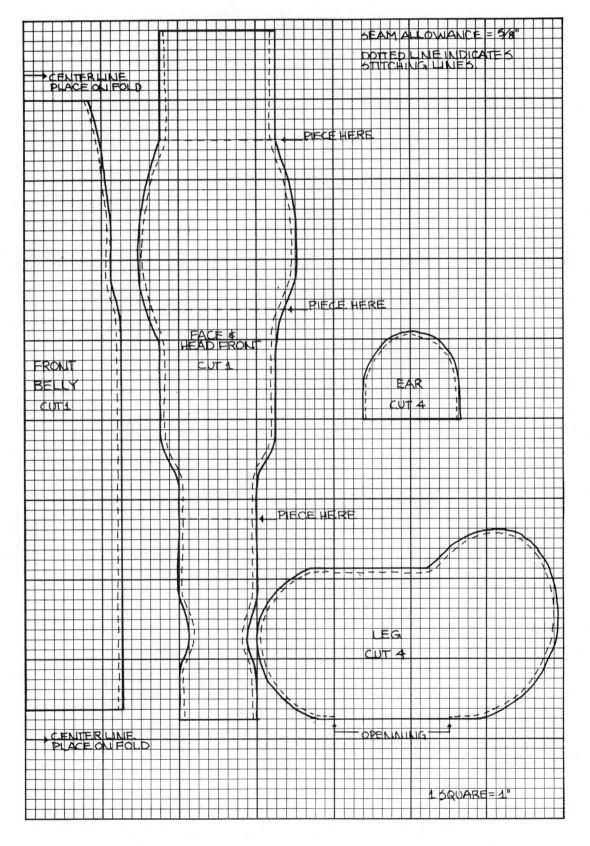

SEAM ALLOWANCE = 5/8"

DOTTED LINE INDICATES
STITCHING LINES

CENTERLINE
PLACE ON FOLD

PIECE HERE

PIECE HERE

FACE &
HEAD FRONT
CUT 1

EAR
CUT 4

FRONT
BELLY

CUT 1

PIECE HERE

LEG
CUT 4

CENTERLINE
PLACE ON FOLD

OPENNING

1 SQUARE = 1"

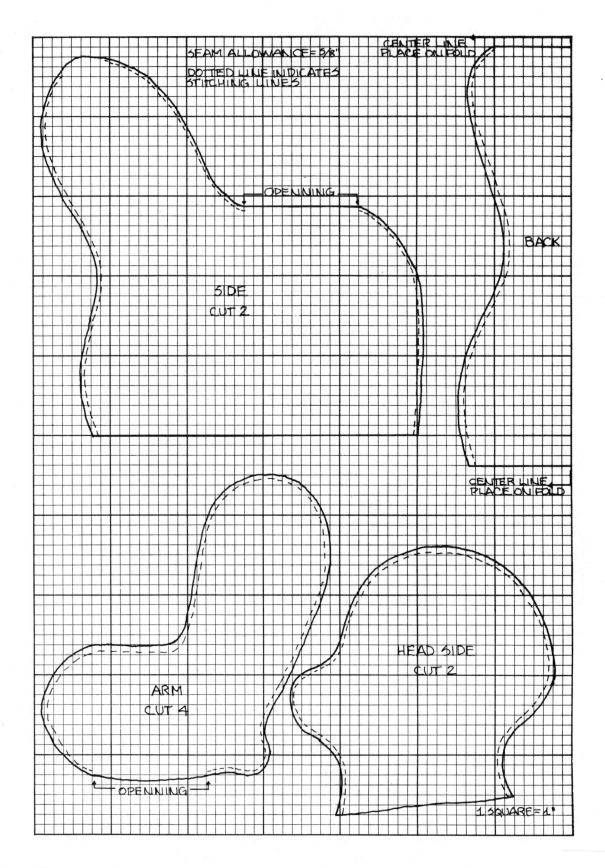

EXTRAS

Everyone knows that life is not complete without "those little things," and this section just fills that void.

Lighting, shelves, boxes, or even a sponge chair that can be used for the shower stall are some of our suggestions. We feel our extras are extra special.

NAME IN LIGHTS

CAROLYN CRAWFORD

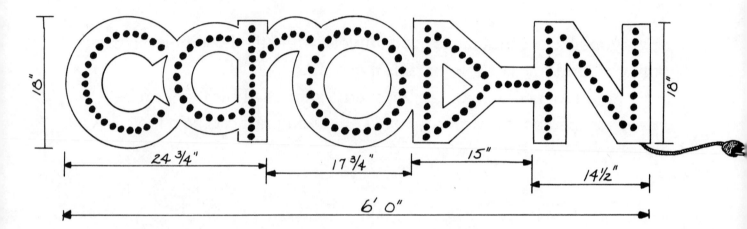

Materials
— **one** piece plywood, ¾″ x 18″ x 6′
— pt. wood stain
— **five** sets of Christmas lights (**twenty** lights per set)
— pencil

Tools
— jigsaw
— drill
— brush, 2″
— staple gun

Method
Examine illustrations
— draw letters on plywood
— using jigsaw, cut around and inside letters
— drill holes through the center of each letter, approximately 1″ apart
— stain wood
— insert Christmas lights (holes must be small enough to hold sockets securely)
— staple excess wire to back of plywood

2 LIGHT FIXTURE

DEBBIE GOLD

Materials

— **one** piece sheet metal, 24″ x 24″ x ⅛′
— **one** piece sheet metal, 20″ x 20″ x ⅛″
— **one** piece sheet metal, 16″ x 16″ x ⅛″
— **one** piece sheet metal, 12″ x 12″ x ⅛″
— **one** piece sheet metal, 8″ x 8″ x ⅛″
— **one** piece sheet metal, 4″ x 4″ x ⅛″
— **one** 18″ circular ceiling fixture with **four** sockets for bulbs
— **one** 6″ long metal rod, 1″ in diameter
— **one** 4 ft. long electrical cord
— red, white, blue, and black cans of spray enamel
— **one** metal thread to fit rod

Tools

— screwdriver
— hammer
— electrical tape for wires in ceiling fixture
— **four** screws to put fixture on the wall

Method

— have a metal shop or factory cut **four**
holes into each plate according to diagram
— have shop as well bore a 1″ hole through center of each plate
— spray metal sheets with enamel according to color preference
— have shop solder metal rod to smallest plate (4″ x 4″), or do it yourself, provided you have proper soldering materials
— twist corresponding sizes of plates on to rod (which is attached to smallest plate), leaving approximately 1″ between each plate
— attach ceiling fixture wires to electric cord; cover bare wires with electrical tape
— attach ceiling fixture to wall using screws, screwdriver, and hammer
— twist rod (which has all the plates attached to it) into hole in center of ceiling fixture

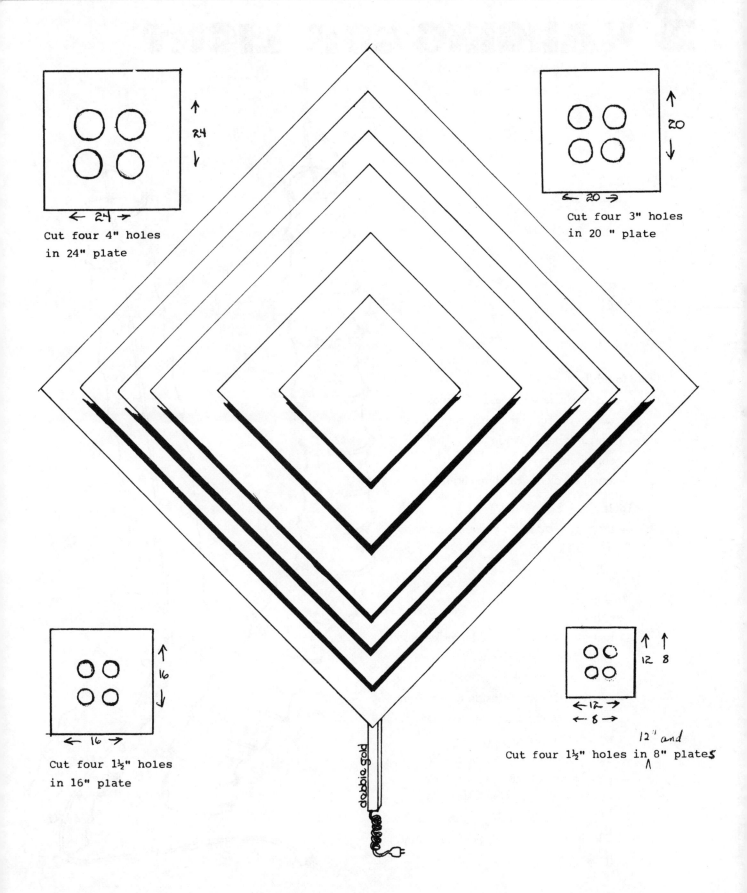

Cut four 4" holes
in 24" plate

Cut four 3" holes
in 20 " plate

Cut four 1½" holes
in 16" plate

Cut four 1½" holes in 8" plates

12" and

dobbie gold

3 HANGING COIL LIGHT

ASE ASK

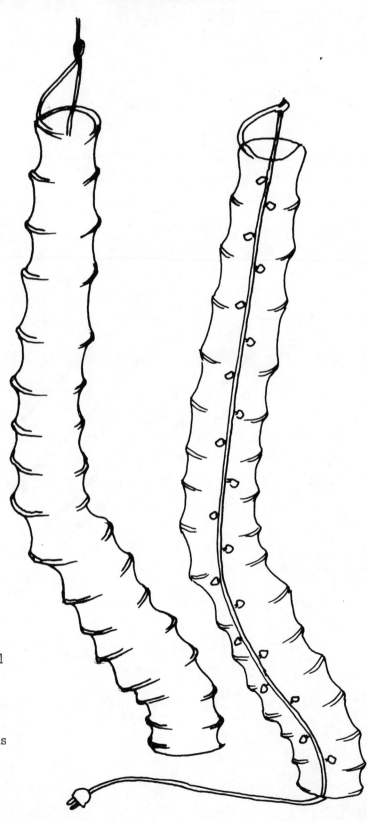

Materials
— **one** roll 30′ steel wire, 1/16″ thick
— **three** yds. tubular translucent white
    stretch fabric, 6″ wide
— ceiling hook
— small set clear Christmas lights

Tools
— large coffee can, to make 8″ diameter
    wire circles
— pliers

Method
Examine illustrations
— using coffee can as guide, make a coil
    of 8″ diameter circles with wire
— cover coil with fabric
— space coils evenly inside the covering
— make a small hook at the top end of coil
    with pliers
— attach wire hook to ceiling hook
— place set of Christmas lights down
    center of covered coil so that plug end is
    at bottom and the opposite end is
    attached to top of coil hook or ceiling
    hook

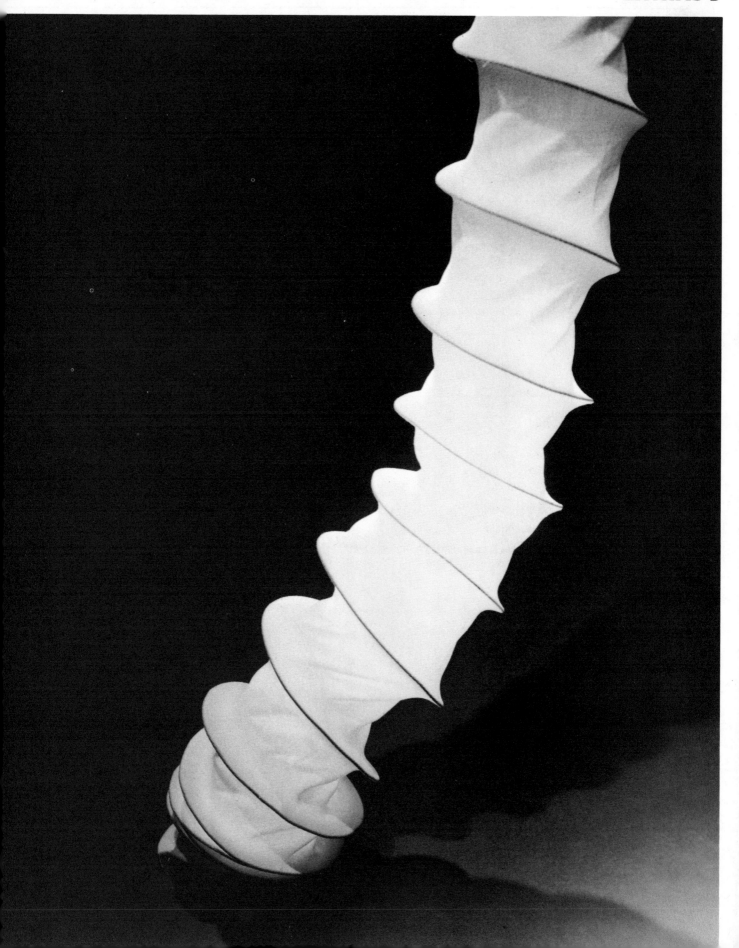

4 MOP ART HANGING LIGHT

SPIROS ZAKAS

Materials

— **one** ceiling hook
— fishing line or thin chain
— **one** wire lamp shade frame
— **two** "Mop Art" mops*
— a few feet of electrical cord
— electric socket
— electric plug
— 25 watt bulb

Tools

— pencil
— knife
— scissors

Method

Examine illustrations
— mark point on ceiling where you wish
  to hang light
— attach ceiling hook to ceiling
— attach fishing line or chain to ceiling

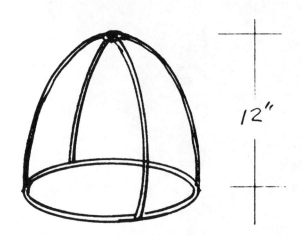

12"

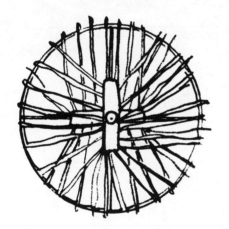

hook; let line or chain dangle from ceiling hook, decide on length and cut
— now crisscross **one** mop over the other mop, over the wire lamp shade frame
— the canvas strap of each mop will be exposed at the top; with a flip of some of the mop strands, cover the canvas straps (concealing the canvas straps)
— place the electrical cord through the finial hole, at top of wire frame
— check the length of your cord so that it reaches the wall outlet
— attach socket to electrical cord and finial hole
— screw in 25 watt bulb
— attach plug to the other end of the electrical cord
— hang covered wire frame light from line attached to ceiling hook
  * Available only from Spiros Zakas, 252 Front Street, N.Y., N.Y. 10038

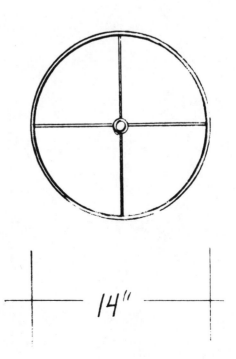

14"

5 HOOP WALL UNIT

BILLY COHEN

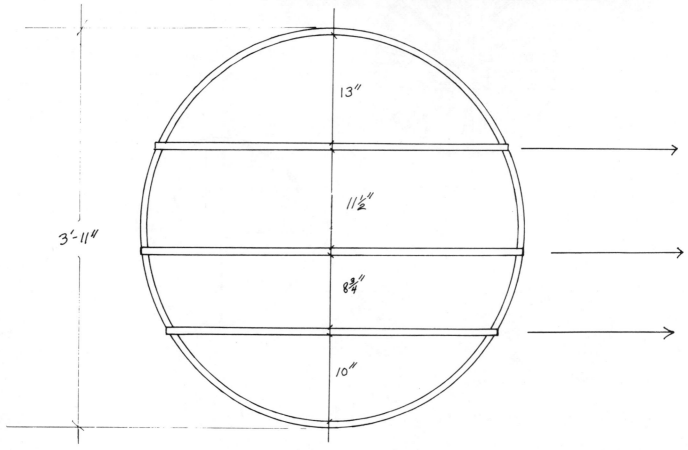

13″

11½″

3′-11″

8¾″

10″

Materials

— **one** round wood canvas stretcher, 47" diameter x ¾" wide x 1" deep
— **one** piece pine board, ¾" thick x 7¼" wide x 11" long
— white glue
— **six** finishing nails, 2"
— plastic wood
— **six** screw-eyes
— **one** qt. primer
— **one** qt. paint

Tools

— saw
— file
— hammer
— sandpaper, fine and medium
— brush, 2" wide

Method

Examine illustrations

— cut ¾" thick pine board into **three** pieces (lengths shown in illustration)
— at both ends of all **three** boards cut out a center piece (see illustration), forming a slot that will fit flush against hoop (use a file to make the angles that correspond to angles of hoop at the **six** points at which shelves intersect hoop)
— place shelves inside hoop; stretch hoop a bit to get the middle shelf in (be careful not to bend too much)
— glue each shelf into place
— hammer a nail through the hoop into each shelf at both ends
— the shelves must fit perfectly against hoop; if there are any spaces, fill them with plastic wood
— screw screw-eyes into the top back of each shelf for hanging on the wall
— sandpaper, prime, paint, and hang

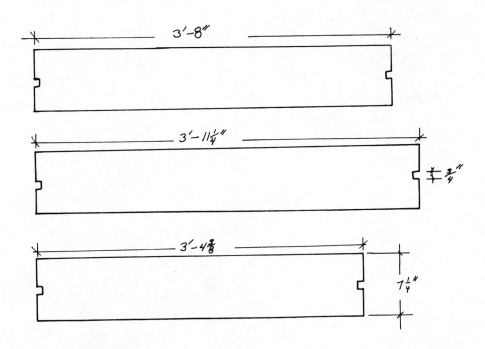

6 BARN WOOD BOX

GREG PETERSEN

Materials
— barn wood, ¾"
— oak, ¾"
— dowels, ¼" and 1/16"
— wood glue

Tools
— clamps
— saw
— chisels
— hinges

Method
Examine illustrations
— glue and clamp parts A, B, C, and D, after making appropriate cuts
— "M" stands for 45° mitre cut
— insert part E into bottom of Frame A, B, C, and D and glue
— insert F into dado slots and glue
— hinge part G into F and D, using dowel glued only into three parts
— using the same basic procedure, construct the top part (no miters, only butt joints)
— mortise and hinge top and bottom

Note: All parts should be doweled ¼" after glue has dried. The top mosaic (wood) is as complicated as you make it. My top is a series of involved cuts, not recommended for the novice. The parts are simply cuts glued to form the correct size, then fitted into the top.

110

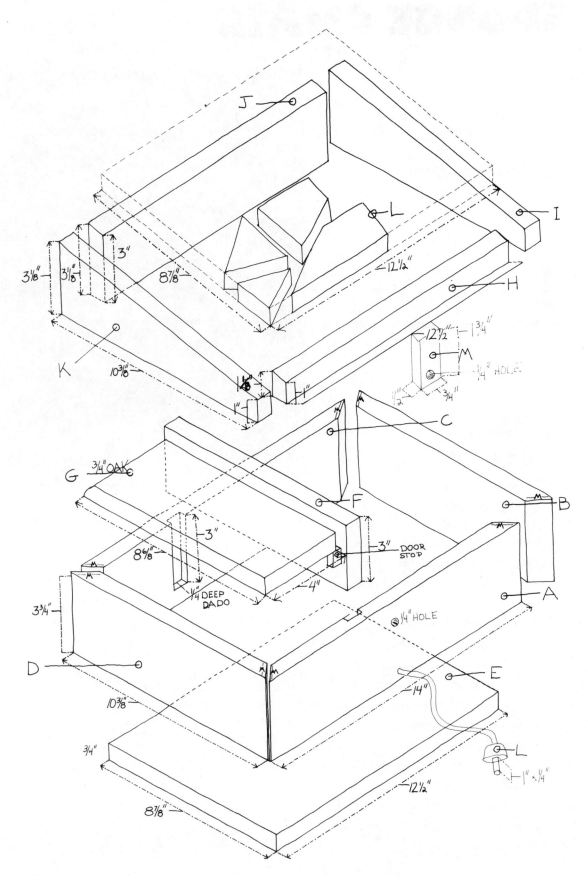

J

I

L

3"

3⅛"   3⅛"

8⅞"

12½"

H

10⅜"

K

12½"   1¾"

M

¼" HOLE

½"   ¾"

C

3/4" OAK

G

F

B

3"

8⅞"

3"

DOOR
STOP

4"

A

¼ DEEP
DADO

¼" HOLE

3¾"

D

E

14"

10⅜"

3/4"

L

1" x ¼"

8⅞"

12½"

7 SPONGE CHAIR

CAROLYN CRAWFORD

Materials

— **one** plastic Parsons table, 16″ x 16″ x 16″
— **ten** large porous sponges, 2½″ x 7″ x 8″
— natural twine
— large bottle white glue

Tools

— single-edged razor blade
— embroidery needle

Method

Examine illustrations

— glue **four** whole sponges on top of
Parsons table, allowing enough room
at rear to insert **two** sponges
— cut remaining sponges into **four** equal
parts, maintaining the dimensions
7″ x 8″, but changing the thickness; each
newly cut sponge is now ⅝″ x 7″ x 8″
— place and glue sponges around the base
of "seat"; you will need to trim away
the excess sponge (the sponges placed
and glued along the base of the "seat"
will be narrow rectangles)
— wrap and glue sponges around the legs
of the table, or "seat"
— thread twine in a large embroidery
needle, and sew together all the seams
between the sponges

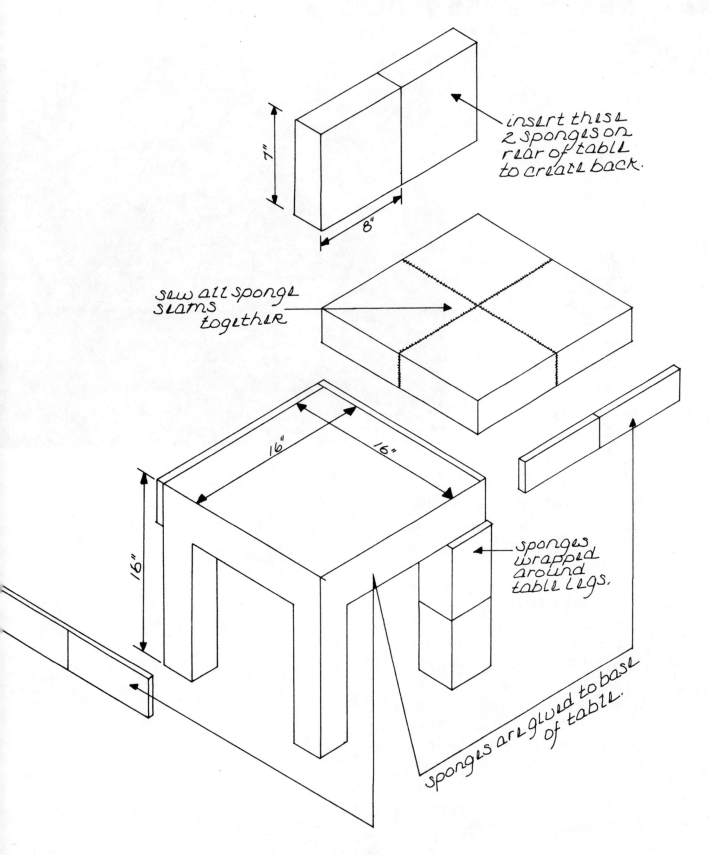

insert these
2 sponges on
rear of table
to create back.

7"

8"

sew all sponge
seams
together

16"

16"

16"

sponges
wrapped
around
table legs.

sponges are glued to base
of table.

8 MOP ART RUG

SPIROS ZAKAS

Materials
— **eight** "Mop Art" mops*
— **eight** rubber bands

Tools
— none needed

Method
— unravel each mop strand
— arrange **eight** mops on a flat surface,
  forming a circular shape, with all **eight**
  canvas straps, from the top of each mop,
  in the center
— connect these **eight** mops to form **one** rug
  by taking a few strands from the
  adjacent mops and braid pigtails
— at the ends of the braided pigtails attach
  a tight-fitting rubber band to hold each
  braid in place, then fluff up the ends

    Note: "Mop Art" mops, made of rayon,
take beautifully to cold water dye. The
photographed rug is an example of the
varied sculptures you can create with
"Mop Art" mops.

    * Available only from Spiros Zakas, 252
Front Street, N.Y., N.Y. 10038

BIG STUFF

Round About Dining, believe it or not, can easily be built in one day. We made it the day before Thanksgiving because we needed to seat twelve people. The only problem we have is that no one ever leaves the dinner table (it is so comfortable). If you are kitchen people as we are—people who like to entertain around the kitchen table—then you and your friends will enjoy Round About Dining.

Depending upon the amount of space you have, you could make a seating unit for four, six, eight, ten, twelve, or fourteen people to sit easily. Because the top is padded and covered in vinyl, it becomes a nice surface to touch and it's perfect for playing games and cards. It's fast to clean and equally easy to change.

FLOATING COMFORT UNITS

SPIROS ZAKAS

Materials (multiply the materials needed by
the number of units desired)
— **one** solid core flush door, 1⅜" x 36" x
84"
— **four** galvanized steel pipes, 1" x 18",
threaded at both ends
— **four** PVC pipes, 4" diameter x 1¾" long
— **eight** 3" diameter steel caplets with 1"
threaded hole
— **sixteen** wood screws, ½"
— **one** polyurethane foam, 3" x 36" x 84"
— **one** piece polyester padding, 1" x 48" x
96"
— **one** piece plush velvet fabric, 50" x 98"

Tools

— pencil
— T square
— drill and bits
— tape measure
— screwdriver
— staple gun
— band saw

Method

Examine illustrations
— mark the **four** points for positioning the
four caplets on the underside of **one** door
— drill ½" deep pilot holes at each mark
— attach **four** caplets to door at these **four**
points; fasten caplets with wood screws
— screw each threaded steel pipe into
each attached caplet
— take the other **four** caplets and screw
them on to the free ends of each steel pipe
— stand the door on its legs
— center foam on the door
— center polyester padding over the foam
— wrap the padding around the foam and
door, bringing its edges under the door;
staple all around the underside
— place plush velvet fabric over the
attached polyester; fold the fabric edges
before stapling it to the underside of
the door so that all the raw edges are
concealed

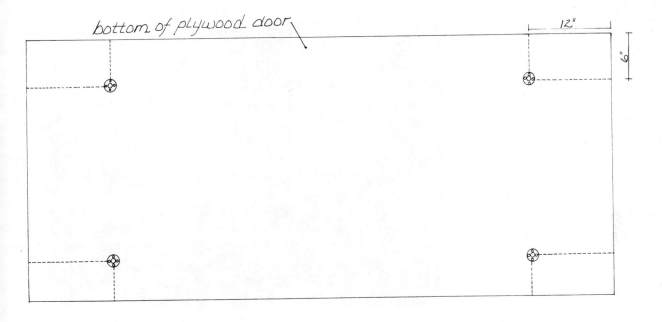

bottom of plywood door

12"

6"

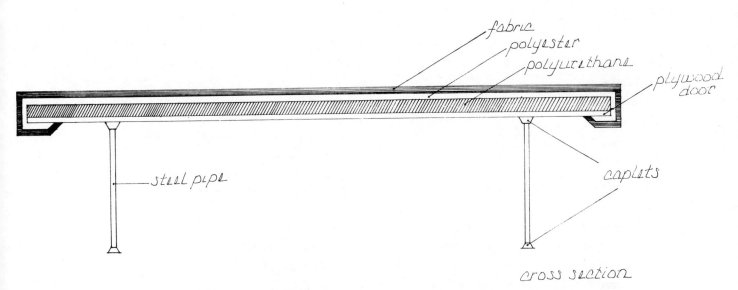

fabric
polyester
polyurethane

plywood
door

steel pipe

caplets

cross section

— decorate the PVC pipes with aluminum
   foil, acrylic paint, fabric, or self-adhering
   paper (comes in solids, colorful prints,
   simulated wood grains, etc.)
— slip PVC pipes over the steel legs
— position your first completed floating
   unit
— repeat the above procedure for each
   additional floating unit

2 ROUND ABOUT DINING

SPIROS ZAKAS

Materials

— **three** sheets plywood, ¾" x 4' x 8'
— **six** pieces wood, 2" x 4" x 8'
— **two** sheets flexible plywood, ¼" x 16" x 27"
— **one** sheet flexible plywood, ¼" x 16" x 152"
— **one** piece hardboard, ¼" x 6" x 152"
— **twelve** 1" x 14" galvanized steel pipes, threaded at both ends
— **five** 1" x 26" galvanized steel pipes, threaded at both ends
— **thirty-four** steel caplets 3" wide, with 1" threaded openings
— cut nails
— common nails
— finishing nails
— ½" wood screws
— bolt polyester padding, 48" wide

— **one** slab polyurethane foam, 4" x 12" x 152"
— **two** slabs polyurethane foam, each 4" x 20" x 96"
— **ten** yds. upholstery material
— 66" square vinyl

Tools

— tape measure
— string
— pencil
— T square
— level
— protractor
— saw horse
— saber saw
— handsaw, to cut 2 x 4s
— hammer
— drill and bits

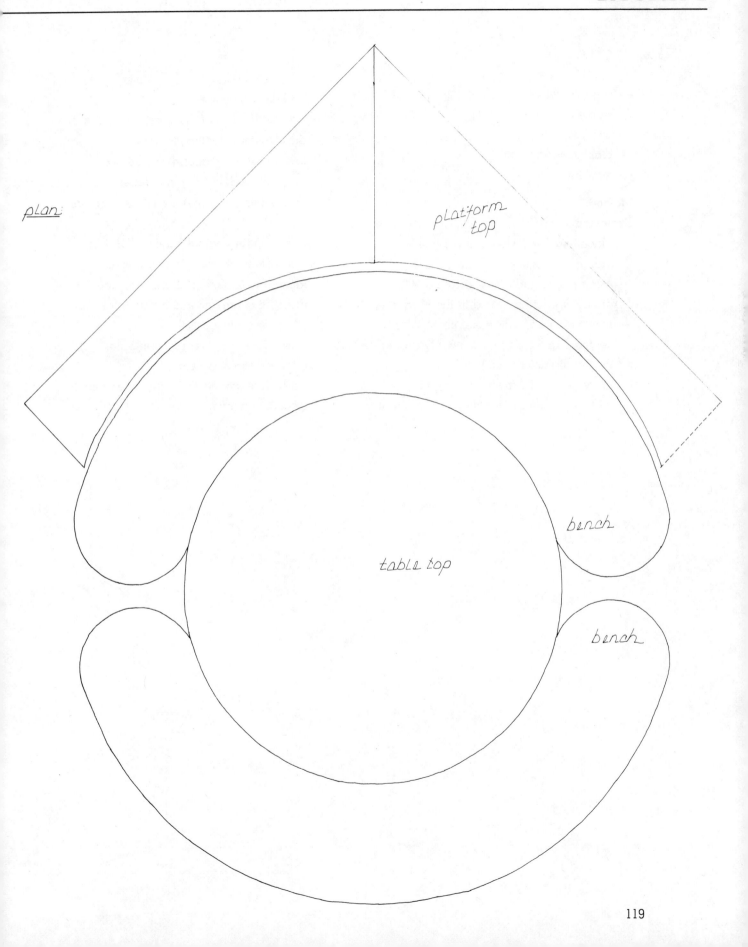

plan:

platform top

bench

table top

bench

— screwdriver
— staple gun
— band saw
— pinking shears
— masking tape

Method

Examine illustrations

— place **two** 4' x 8' sheets side by side, forming a 8' square
— using pencil and string, scribe a 60" diameter circle centered in the 8' square
— now scribe a 96" diameter circle, also centered in the 8' square (evenly around the 60" diameter circle)
— draw pattern for the bench ends by making a semicircle with a 9" radius at

each bench end
— take third sheet of plywood, ¾" x 4' x 8'
— draw patterns for the platform
— to support the platform, secure **six** vertical 2 x 4s x 23½" to corner walls
— secure **two** horizontal 2 x 4s x 8' to corner walls
— secure **eight** vertical 2 x 4s x 26¾" to front edges of **two** platform pieces
— fasten **two** table top pieces together
— attach **five** caplets to the bottom of the plywood table top
— screw **five** 26" steel pipes into the attached table caplets
— screw **five** caplets to the free end of each steel pipe above

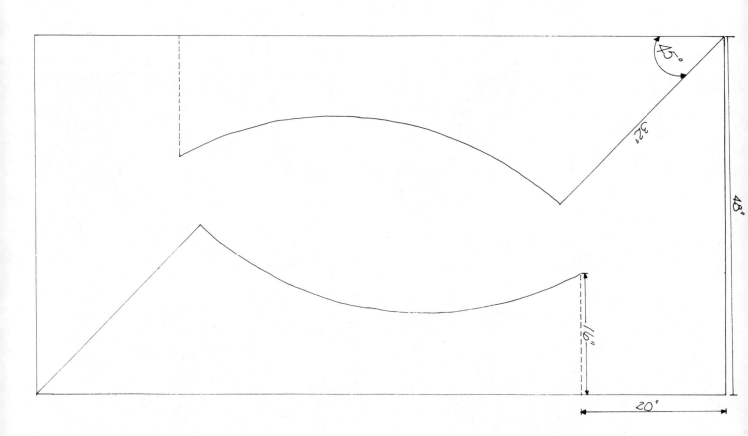

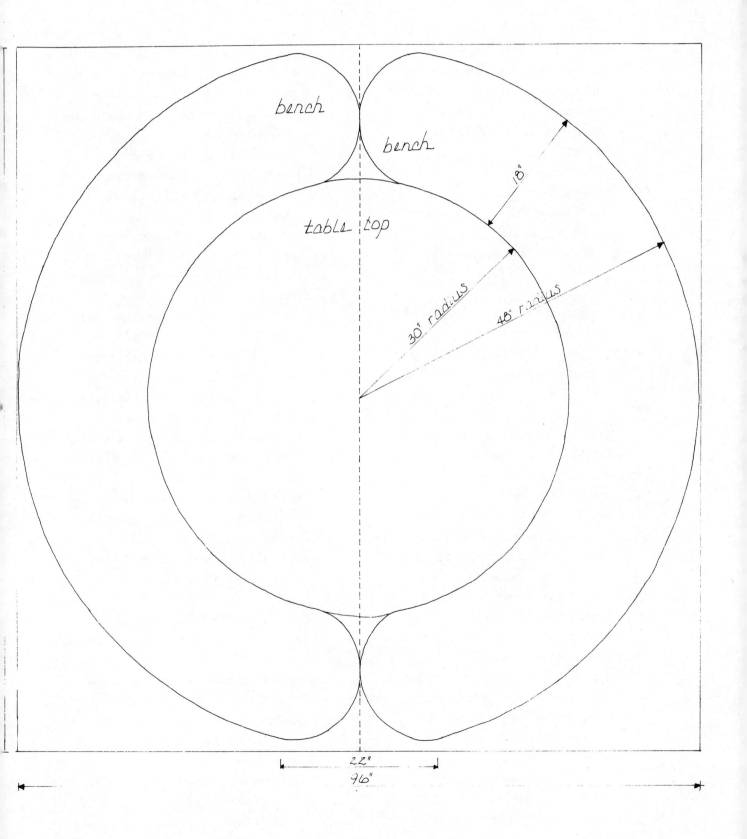

bench

bench

table top

18"

30" radius

48" radius

22"
96"

— stand table on its **five** legs
— take **two** bench pieces and position **six** caplets on each bench piece at 18″ intervals
— attach these **six** caplets to **two** bench pieces
— screw **twelve** 13″ steel pipes into the attached bench caplets
— screw **twelve** caplets to the free end of each steel pipe above
— stand **two** benches on its legs

To Upholster
— cut a piece of polyester padding to fit the platform shape, allow 2″ overlaps at the ends and front edge of platform
— use staple gun to staple the padding to the back edges of the platform, then pull and staple the padding underneath the ends and front edges of platform
— cut the upholstery fabric; this time allow a 4″ overlap at the ends, front edges, and back edges
— fold along the 4″ margin of fabric, place the fold along the back edge of the platform, lift the fabric and staple fabric to the top back edge of the platform along the **inside** (wrong side) fold of fabric (fabric which is attached to platform has a smooth appearance and all stapes are concealed)
— take the fabric and staple to underside of platform at the ends and in front
— to form a back support for a polyurethane bolster, use the hardboard piece
— cover the hardboard piece with 1″ x 10″ x 156″ piece of polyester padding; staple to the back of hardboard

— with piece of fabric 12″ x 158″, cover the hardboard piece, attaching the fabric only to the back of the top edge of hardboard piece; position the hardboard to the curve of the platform
— lift the fabric covering the hardboard piece and nail the hardboard piece to the front edge of the platform
— fold 4″ x 12″ x 152″ piece of polyurethane foam in half lengthwise; keep the fold at the top; position foam against the hardboard piece (under the padding and fabric)
— drop the padding and fabric over the polyurethane foam, and staple padding and fabric to back of hardboard piece at both ends and bottom
— to cover both open ends of the platform, cut **two** ¼″ x 16″ x 27″ pieces of hardboard; cover each piece of wood with a piece of fabric 18″ x 29″ (these panels remain unpadded)
— use finishing nails to secure these panels to the 2 x 4s at each end of the platform structure
— cover the table top with vinyl fabric; staple to underside of table top all around
— cut a 4″ x 20″ x 96″ piece of polyurethane foam for each bench; place on top of each bench
— cover each bench top and foam with 1″ x 24″ x 100″ polyester padding; staple in place
— cut a piece of fabric for each bench, 24″ x 100″
— cover each bench with fabric, pulling and stapling the fabric to the underside of each bench

MATERIALS AND TOOLS

Materials are the things that go into a product and tools are the things that come out. For example, the hammer is a tool and plywood the material. It's really important to gather the materials and tools together before you begin. What usually makes things difficult is not having the proper tools and materials when you need them to do the job.

Many of today's lumberyards have begun looking more like supermarkets, complete with shopping carts, and you can get almost everything you need in one. This type of lumberyard is not usually found in the city, so you will have to go to the suburbs for one-store shopping.

There are generally six sources for obtaining the materials and tools for these projects, although it's quite possible to find most if not all of what you need at a single source.

Art supply stores: Carry the straight edges (or T squares), marking tools, acrylic tube paints, brushes, circle templates, compasses, cardboard, paint, primers, rubber cement, Exacto knives, etc.

Fabric supply stores: Obviously they carry fabrics but also scissors, pinking shears, needles, pins, fabric markers, pattern paper, zippers, Ultra-suede, embroidery thread, felt, crewel needles, etc.

Hardware stores: Carry belt sanders, table saws, drill presses, hammers, screwdrivers, "C" clamps, putty knives, plastic wood filler, clothes lines, nail punches, electrical wiring and sockets, etc.

Hobby stores: Carry various glues, Teddy bear eyes, balsam wood, Testers enamel paints, spray glue, foam core, styrofoam, casein glue, various game pieces, fine sandpaper, Magic Markers, etc.

Lumberyards: Carry plywoods of all thicknesses, 2 x 4s, 1 x 2s, and 1 x 3s, etc. This is also a good source for all wood screws, hinges, screening nails, Plexi-glass, closet pole, dowel, wire braid, etc.

Upholstery suppliers: Carry polyurethane foam in all thicknesses, foam rubber (which is similar to polyurethane but twice as costly), polyester for soft edges over the polyurethane, tacks, staple guns and staples, sewing machine accessories, etc.

Now that you know where to get the supplies you can begin a new creative hobby that functions in more ways than one.

DESCRIPTIONS

acrylic paint   plastic-based paint

band saw   saw that is shaped like a rubber band and moves around clockwise

barn wood   wood that has been weathered

belt sander   sandpaper that is shaped like a rubber band and revolves

bit   piece of metal shaped like a headless nail and used for drilling

bolster   shaped like a hot dog and is equally soft; its size is the width of a bed

bolt   metal piece that works like a screw but is much larger

clamps   pieces of metal that can be placed on two opposite ends very tightly

caplet   a piece usually made of metal that holds a rod

casein white glue   probably more commonly known as Elmer's or Sobo glue; it is made from milk

chisel   tool that is shaped at one end like a ruler; used for removing thin layers of wood

circle template   flat piece of plastic that has various circles cut out of it

circular saw   saw that is shaped like a record with saw teeth on the rim

circular table saw   circular saw set into a table

cleat   like a bracket used to hold two pieces together

coping saw   tool with a very thin (ice-pick size) blade used for cutting

cotton velour   fabric that looks like velvet and feels more like cordless corduroy

countersink   to recess a nail or screw below the surface

crossbar   piece of metal or wood used to hold together two other pieces

dado   rectangular groove

dimmer   small plastic unit with a large button shape on it that turns the wattage down on light bulbs

dowel   round piece of wood shaped like a pencil

dress   to cover or paint a piece of wood or to cover the natural surface

drill press   drill that moves up and down by means of a lever

elbow   piece of metal that connects two pieces on any angle

Exacto knife   has thin sharp blade that fits on a pencil shape

epoxy   two resins which when combined become an adhesive

eye screw   screw with a circle on the end

fabric marker   thin soap, like a marker, that makes a removable mark on fabric

fiberglass   thin hairlike strands of glass

finial hole   small hole into which things are screwed

flathead wood screw   screw that is flat on top with a groove in it

flexible plywood   thin plywood that can be bent

galvanized steel pipes   heavy pipes used

for hot and cold water

grid bunch of lines that are shaped into equal boxes that can represent a point of reference for measuring

groove long insert or channel

hex head screw with a hexangular indentation on the head

L-shaped metal bracket corner piece that holds together two other pieces

latex paint paint with a rubber base that mixes with water and cleans that way too

mallet heavy piece of metal that is used like a hammer for heavy hammering

masking tape tape made of paper that is easily removable

Masonite hard smooth board made of small particles of wood and glue

miter an angle

miter box box used for obtaining a consistent angle many times

nail punch small round piece of metal that looks like a pencil with a dull point

nuts flat, small pieces of metal shaped like squares and hexangles that fit on a screw

oak heavy grained wood

piano hinge long, narrow hinge that closes flat

pine soft, largely grained wood

pinking shears scissors that have saw teeth on their blades

piping soft (sipping straw shape) piece of cotton that is used for highlighting seams

plane tool that flattens out wood

plastic wood synthetic claylike substance that is used to fill in small openings in wood

plywood three or more layers of veneer (cross grained) glued together

polyester fiber fiber that is usually white; a synthetic plastic polyester fiber

primer paint that helps seal the pores of the surface

protractor drafting tool that makes accurate circles

push pin pin with a big plastic or metal head on the end

putty knife utensil that is soft and pliable with no sharp edges

P.V.C. plastic piping synthetic pipes that are used for plumbing

riser a vertical surface that meets with a horizontal one

seam allowance enough fabric left on the edges so two pieces of fabric can be sewn together

Scotch Guard trade name for a synthetic coating that makes fabric more liquid-resistant

screen mold frame of window screen

stud vertical support

tongue something that protrudes

Ultra-Suede trade name for synthetic fabric that looks and feels like suede

valance horizontal piece that is on top

veneer thin sheet form of wood

washer metal piece that looks like a life-saver and feels like a dime

white railroad board cardboard that is glued with a sheet of white paper on one side